THE WESTMINSTER SOURCE BOOKS
FOR MINISTERS

PASTORAL WORK

THE WESTMINSTER SOURCE BOOKS
FOR MINISTERS

Memorial Service .25

2.00

2.00

THE FUNERAL, by Andrew W. Blackwood
THE CHRISTIAN SACRAMENTS, by Hugh Thomson Kerr
PASTORAL WORK, by Andrew W. Blackwood

(Other volumes in preparation)

PASTORAL WORK

A Source Book for Ministers

ANDREW WATTERSON BLACKWOOD
Chairman of the Practical Department
The Theological Seminary, Princeton, New Jersey

PHILADELPHIA

THE WESTMINSTER PRESS

PRINTED IN THE UNITED STATES OF AMERICA

Acknowledgments

FRIENDS near and far have helped me in preparing to write. The following deserve special thanks: George M. Harper, Ph.D., Woodrow Professor of Literature, emeritus, Princeton University; the Rev. James C. Perkins, pastor of the First Congregational Church, Niagara Falls, New York; the Rev. David Davids, pastor of Summit Congregational Church, Dubuque, Iowa; and the friends at The Pastors' School in Southern Methodist University, Dallas, Texas. As for my students of yesterday and today here at Princeton, the number of my helpers has been legion.

The following have kindly granted me permission to quote. All the publications except the first are subject to copyright:

The Rev. George A. Buttrick, D.D.
> *A Guide for the Church Visitor,* issued privately by the
> Madison Avenue Presbyterian Church, New York

The Century Company
> *The Making of a Minister,* by former Dean Charles R.
> Brown

Harper and Brothers
> *Clerical Errors,* by Lewis Tucker

J. B. Lippincott Company
> *Old Soldiers Never Die* and *The Night Is Ending,* both
> by James Ronald

Charles Scribner's Sons
> *The Poems of Henry van Dyke*

The Westminster Press
> *The Significance of the Cross,* by F. W. Dillistone

CONTENTS

PART ONE

Basic Forms of Pastoral Work

CONTENTS

PART TWO

Other Kinds of Pastoral Work

Foreword

THE request for this book has come from various pastors. After I sent out my work on *The Funeral*, parish ministers began writing to ask me for something of the sort about pastoral work today. Similar appeals have come at ministerial conferences. Clergymen everywhere seem to be perplexed about things pastoral. They would agree with the late Dean William Adams Brown. One of his last books included a discussion of theological education. In the light of current surveys he declared that our chief weakness has lain in pastoral theology.[1] Evidently our teaching has been theoretical and hortatory, not practical and helpful. Instead of dealing with cases, methods, and ideals, we have often presented " practical theology " impractically.

Such a weakness may have been due to the difficulty of the undertaking. The time allotted has been little. The medical student normally has devoted to clinical work the last two years in school, with an additional internship at a hospital. His brother in the seminary has been exposed to things practical in a few minor courses. The instruction has often consisted of theoretical lectures, venerable enough to be retired on a pension. The clinical training, if any, may have been given at a home for the feeble-minded. What a queer preparation for pastoral work! Such conditions, however, are being remedied.

" What we need, apparently, is some technical literature, specializing on the details of the minister's life, and the everyday demands of his office." [2] Thus Dr. Lloyd C. Douglas wrote while he served as a parish minister. More recently such volumes have been coming forth. Still there seems to be a demand for something more. The resulting aim here is practical. The method calls for the use of cases from life. The theories also have grown out of experience. Every proposal has come from the field. The practical philosophy is not that of an arm-chair dreamer.

As a teacher I have studied the literature of the subject, beginning with the Old Testament. I have learned much from the sort of biography and fiction that appears in the Appendix. I have watched master shepherds at work among flocks large and small. I have likewise drawn freely from my own experience. Beginning with my boyhood in the home of a " horse-and-buggy doctor," the Lord has led me into almost every kind of field except among the fabulously rich. Gradually I have evolved a working philosophy. It concerns the things that should matter most in the work of a parish minister.

The time in view is one of rebuilding after World War II. The clergyman before us has ability and charm, as well as training. To what should he give the priority? Let him strive to excel in pastoral work, in public prayer, and in preaching. On the human level nothing else appears to me so vital. Such an " all-round minister " is much in demand today. Why should any local church have to seek far for a man with a shepherd heart who can preach and pray? Fortunately, anyone called of God to the parish ministry can learn to become a good pastor. The question is, How?

ANDREW WATTERSON BLACKWOOD.

The Theological Seminary,
Princeton, New Jersey.

PART ONE

Basic Forms of Pastoral Work

I

The Rediscovery of the Need

MANY a minister has recently discovered the importance of
pastoral work. Together with public worship, which includes
preaching, the care of souls has become the chief concern of
such a parish leader. For a generation or two many clergymen
strove to discover acceptable substitutes for the pastoral nurture of people, one by one and by households. In large measure
we failed. We feel that most of those other activities have their
places in the local church. But now we know that nothing sec-
ondary can absolve the minister from his God-given privilege
of shepherding the flock, including stray sheep.

Such a message comes from sources near and far. One summer, for instance, Dr. George A. Buttrick, noteworthy as pastor and preacher, spoke for a week in Dallas, Texas. He was
addressing a host of ministers, the majority of them young and
many of them rural. The metropolitan divine said in part:
" You can never build up a strong congregation solely by
preaching. You must go to the people yourself. You build up
a spiritual church by wearing out shoe leather and automobile tires. You can hold it together by worthy preaching."
Those Methodist auditors might have responded with fervent
" Amens." Since they did not, perhaps they were too busy
searching their hearts.

During that summer school, the writer conducted two
classes in homiletics. At the close of the session he was invited
to return the following year and give a course on " How to Do
Pastoral Work Today." Note the stress on that stubborn old
word, How? Indirectly, that request from Texas friends has
led to the present volume. Before we turn to the subject, however, let us think further about the rediscovery of the need.
What has brought about the shift in emphasis? Since the dis-

cussion must be limited, the treatment will be suggestive, not exhaustive.

1. *"The Return to Religion."* This current movement may not be so widespread and auspicious as we sometimes suppose. Only coming generations can tell. At present who will deny that there has been among us a growing concern about religion? For example, consider the revival of emphasis on Christian doctrine. Present-day thinkers may have contributed little to our understanding of God. But they have delved deeply into revealed truth about man. For example, Professor Reinhold Niebuhr writes about *The Nature and Destiny of Man.* In the Bible such teachings often relate to the individual. Herein lies one of the basic ideals in pastoral theology. The worth of the individual!

There has likewise been a renewal of concern about the use of the Bible. The major stress rightly falls on the New Testament. That brings out the importance of the individual, as well as " the Ecumenical Church." Listen to an eloquent exponent of the Social Gospel, the late Francis G. Peabody, of the Divinity School at Harvard. He says that the teachings of Jesus " begin with the individual." " His Kingdom is to come, not by outward force or social organization, . . . but by the progressive sanctification of individual human souls." [1] That seems to call for pastoral care, including personal evangelism.

2. *The Stress on the Individual.* Somewhat recently Dr. Buttrick has written about the relation between " Preaching Christ to the Social Order " and " Preaching Christ to the Individual." These chapter headings appear in a book about homiletics. Note the mastery of the written word: " If religion ends with the individual, it ends. Verily. But if it does not begin with the individual, it never begins, and has no being. . . . The seed of all things human is selfhood." [2] This too points the way toward pastoral nurture.

Professor H. H. Farmer, of Cambridge, England, speaks from a point of view quite different. His wise little book [3] deals with the relation between Christian doctrine and preaching.

" The Gospel is a Gospel of succour and challenge to the individual soul. . . . It is God's word to man as man, whatever his situation, whatever the external setting of his life. We must ask, and expect in the name of Christ, the response of decision and trust and obedience in the individual, who must in the end settle the matter in the private places of his own heart." Elsewhere in this heart-searching book the theologian declares, " Preaching is essentially a pastoral activity." In short, leading thinkers may differ much about other things, but many are alike in the rediscovery of the individual. This New Testament truth lies at the heart of pastoral theology.

Much the same emphasis appears in a recent best seller, by no means religious. In the forty-seventh edition of *Man, the Unknown*,[4] Dr. Alexis Carrel devotes one eighth of his volume to a chapter on " The Individual." The writer draws a strong contrast between " human beings," who are scientific abstractions, and " the individual," " who acts, suffers, fights, and dies." " Modern society ignores the individual. It only takes account of human beings." " We have treated the individual as a chemical substance, a machine, or a part of a machine." Hence the author pleads for " the remaking of man." Unfortunately, Dr. Carrel holds out no reason for hope. He thinks that man must remake himself, without regard to the One who alone is able to transform both the " world and the individual."

3. *The Importance of the Home.* At least in theory we church folk have begun to rediscover the central importance of the Christian home. It lies close to the heart of all our religion, at least on the human level. Here again, we are simply returning to the ideals of Holy Writ. According to the Bible, our religion started in a home on earth and will culminate with a home in heaven. Especially since 1917, when the Russians tried to do away with the Christian family, many of us have looked on the home as the chief institutional gift of Christianity to the world. Now we rejoice to see that Russia is making an about-face. As in France of old, the leaders of Russia since

the Revolution are finding that the nation needs both the church and the home.

Why should we in the United States cast stones at Russia? Are we not alarmed by the growth of our own juvenile delinquency? For example, Professor Howard McClusky, from the University of Michigan, recently addressed a throng of educators assembled in New York City. He reported the results of a current survey in the junior high school at Battle Creek. Not including families where the parents have been separated temporarily by war work, the survey showed that out of 660 boys and girls, 221 came from broken homes.[5]

Then the professor declared, " We shall soon have another lost generation of wandering tramps — the boys and girls of America." Our students from Michigan do not question these statistics. However, they feel that in other cities, such as Grand Rapids, the findings would not prove so disheartening. In the latter city the home influences and the church life seem to be much more nearly ideal. Evidently the parents and the ministers working together have helped to keep many homes from going on the rocks. In other wartime regions, countless people ignore the central importance of the Christian home.

How can we have streams in the valleys if we permit the springs to run dry on the mountains? Any workable theory of reaching the home religiously calls for intensive pastoral nurture. Spiritually, the present-day family almost never responds to " absent treatment." As Dr. Buttrick told the Texas pastor, " You must go yourself! " That is what he and his associate clergymen do among many homes surrounding the Madison Avenue Presbyterian Church on the East Side of New York City. The same plan will work anywhere in Arkansas or Maine.

During the past year the reunited Methodist Church has inaugurated a movement that should point the way to other branches of disjointed Protestantism. Under the leadership of the bishops, our Wesleyan brethren have begun to emphasize evangelism in the homes of the local parish. Instead of relying chiefly on huge mass meetings, or on sheer individualism, those farsighted statesmen have been stressing the work of the local pastor, and the need of winning the family. " The promise is unto you, and to your children." It has been said that Methodist doctrine proceeds from " the transfiguration of the Christian home." If so, it is fitting that these brethren should stress the family as the unit in parish evangelism. According to various reports, the results of the movement have proved gratifying. Religion in the home!

4. *The Influence of Psychology.* For two generations and more, the modern child has been educated, or half educated, psychologically. Among people of culture today, psychology seems to have displaced logic. Recent exponents of psychology have thrown more and more stress on the individual. Over in Europe a leading advocate of newer ideas has termed his movement " Individual Psychology." Much as some of us dread psychiatry, when divorced from Christ, we should learn from its advocates the wisdom of dealing with one case at a time. That lone person may require hour after hour, at frequent intervals. Only by careful study of the patient can one decide on the treatment.

Every minister ought to read with care an able, disquieting volume from C. G. Jung, of Switzerland.[6] Toward the end he declares: " During the past thirty years people from all parts of the civilized world have consulted me. I have treated many hundreds of patients, the larger number being Protestants, a smaller number Jews, and only five or six believing Catholics. Among all my patients in the second half of life — that is to say, over thirty-five — there has not been one whose problem in the last resort has not been that of finding a religious outlook on life."

Jung reports that such patients " flatly refuse to consult the clergyman." They feel that the typical parson cares little about disorders of the soul, and that he can do nothing to help. Fortunately, many a Protestant minister has determined to remedy this situation. Alas, he scarcely knows how to begin. One thing he ought to remember: The Lord understands every heart

He has made. He is waiting to lead His servant who wishes to acquire a " healing presence." " If any man will do his will, he shall know of the doctrine " (John 7:17). Such willingness to do God's will calls for a vast deal of work. There can be no quick and easy way of dealing with disorders of the soul.

5. *The Concern About the Cults.* In almost every city Protestant pastors have been perplexed by the falling away of church members to certain " new religions." [7] In the United States such societies keep increasing, largely because of accessions from Protestant congregations. Whatever the shortcomings of these movements, surely they devote unlimited attention to the soul disorders that flourish among our people, individually. What Jung writes about the mental state of people in Europe holds true on our side of the water. More than half the hospital rooms in the United States are filled with mental cases.

In many lives today, says Jung, there is " an alarming lack of balance. We are living undeniably in a period of the greatest restlessness, nervous tension, confusion, and deterioration of outlook." If so, is it not time for the parish minister to become concerned about the increasing number of disordered souls? Of course his mode of treatment should differ from that of the cults. Once again we face that old question, How? How minister to the friend in distress of soul — the man who has not yet broken down? Either he will secure relief through the local church or else he will hie away to one of the " new religions." In short, let us quit throwing stones and start cleaning house.

6. *The By-Products of the War.* The typical pastor has been showing praiseworthy concern for the young men and women enrolled in the armed forces. Such pastoral solicitude reaches out to include their loved ones here at home. Our chaplains too are rendering noble service as pastoral counselors. Without daring to pose as a seer, one ventures to hope that when these younger ministers return to parish work they will keep on caring for the souls of men, one by one. Much to his

amazement, many a chaplain has discovered that his chief opportunity for advancing the Kingdom comes in dealing with the man who needs a friend.

This war is not the first that has led to increased emphasis on pastoral care. Someday a lover of books and men will write a history of pastoral work. He will make clear that the ebb and flow of such concern has had much to do with the coming of war and its trail of sorrow. In the churches of Scotland and England, for example, he will find lofty traditions of pastoral nurture. One reason may be that those countries have often sent their sons out to die on land or sea. In the United States also, many of the noblest pastors have served during days of war and so-called " reconstruction." For example, think of Phillips Brooks in Boston and Theodore L. Cuyler in Brooklyn.

In the bloodiest and bitterest period of American history thus far, many a loving pastor learned how to comfort his friends in fear and in grief. When has there ever been more need of comfort than now? Surely the coming decade should witness the rise of pastors who excel in binding up the broken heart and strengthening the feeble soul.

We have glanced at six elements that enter into the present concern about things pastoral. To certain ministers the resulting " discovery " may seem epoch-making. This point of view seems not to be common among leading laymen. They have not changed their minds. With some exceptions church officers and their wives have long been yearning for a shift of ministerial emphasis. They have been wishing for undershepherds who will love the sheep and the lambs, especially the ones in distress. When these lay friends tell us about their ministers of other years, the praise of the lips may concern the pulpit orator, such as Henry Ward Beecher, but the love of the heart goes out to the gentle shepherd, like Theodore L. Cuyler.

As an object lesson of pastoral work, read about Cuyler, who was by no means brilliant. This friend and neighbor of Beecher over in Brooklyn assures us that any man called of God can learn how to excel in the care of souls: " The humblest minister can become a faithful and successful pastor. God never intended that this world should be saved by pulpit geniuses, or else He would have created more of them. . . . Every herald of the Gospel who loves his Master, loves the Bible, loves his fellow men, and hungers to win souls to the Saviour, can become a good pastor, if he honestly tries." [8]

The question remains, How? Since the days of Cuyler and Brooks has there been much change in pastoral methods? More than a little, it seems, but not so much, perhaps, as there will be during the years that follow World War II. The chief change ought to be a still larger increase of emphasis!

Suggested Readings

Calkins, Raymond, *The Romance of the Ministry*. The Pilgrim Press, 1944.

Dicks, Russell L., *Pastoral Work and Personal Counseling*. The Macmillan Company, 1944.

Waterhouse, Eric S., *Psychology and Pastoral Work*. Abingdon-Cokesbury Press, 1940.

Weston, Sidney R., *Ideals of Love and Marriage*. The Macmillan Company, 1944.

II

The Minister After the War

IN times of war and rebuilding the home pastor may develop an inferiority complex. The attention of the religious world has rightly been fixed on the work of chaplains. As the father of one and the teacher of many, the writer believes in that heroic service. He also feels that the Protestant Church should not ignore the men at the home base. Under God, the welfare of the world tomorrow will depend largely on local pastors, including recent seminary graduates. How, then, have they been faring?

At a seminary commencement in wartime suppose that three fourths of the graduates had accepted calls to parish churches. The others planned to go out as chaplains. During the exercises would anyone on the platform have shown any concern about those prospective pastors? In the " free prayers " would anyone have referred to them and their prosaic tasks? Probably not! Fortunately, God cares for the unspectacular. He must have caused these words to be written for our learning: " As his part is that goeth down to the battle, so shall his part be that tarrieth by the stuff " (I Sam. 30:24). What, then, does He expect of the humble servant who remains at home and engages in the humdrum duties of the undershepherd? By way of a tentative answer let us think of the local pastor in terms of war: " Thou therefore endure hardness, as a good soldier of Jesus Christ " (II Tim. 2:3). The apostle addressed these words to a young man called of God to serve as a pastor. What kind of spiritual equipment does such a minister need today?

1. The local pastor should be as *brave as a chaplain*. Occasionally a parish minister has an opportunity to display heroism. Almost without exception the dominie rises to the challenge of peril. Early in his famous ministry Charles H. Spurgeon

21

tarried with the flock during a plague of typhus fever, which swept through the parish in South London. Partly because of those pastoral labors, rendered without favoritism or fear, Spurgeon won the hearts of countless people in that community and far beyond. Some such spirit must have animated the local clergy in the lands recently devastated by war. If so, their names are written bright in heaven.

After World War I, Cardinal Désiré Joseph Mercier came across the Atlantic to receive an honorary degree at Princeton University. To that primate from Belgium, as the hero of invasion days, Dean Andrew F. West presented a copy of a letter written by Saint Augustine. When the barbarians were laying North Africa waste, the bishop of Hippo wrote the parish clergy a letter of cheer, as well as warning. He told them frankly that it would be wrong to close the parish churches and sinful for the shepherds to flee from their flocks. Such a heroic spirit makes one think of Pastor Martin Niemoeller.

As a rule, however, " the romance of the ministry " appears chiefly in the title of an excellent book. Even in the chaplaincy, or on the foreign field, life often proves far from thrilling. In the words of a young Navy chaplain, writing to his friends in the home parish: " Being scared is slightly preferable to being bored. I have been both." More seriously, he told his friends at the Christmas season: " In hundreds of conversations, in foxholes and dugouts, in blackout rooms and sick-bays, in Higgins boats and jeeps, I have come to a strange conclusion. Men with Christian faith are able to hope, and men without faith are not. Hope in the hearts of men who believe is intimately tied up with the events of the first Christmas Day. . . . Christ did not come to make life easy, but to make men strong, in a world where One like Jesus could be crucified. . . . It takes a lot of dive bombers to worry a man who really believes."

All the while there must be different brands of courage. As Woodrow Wilson used to insist, when speaking out of sad experience, " It may prove harder to do your duty when men are

sneering at you than when they are shooting at you." What
sort of vulgar treatment does many a young pastor receive in
days of war and reconstruction? " You look hale and hearty!
Why didn't you enter the army, and help win the war? " Such
sneers constitute no small measure of a pastor's cross. Still he
must stay by the stuff. If he does not, what will become of the
local church?

Many clergymen have been called to the chaplaincy; others
have not. Some are being singled out for missionary service in
China; others should tarry at home. Only the Lord can tell any
minister where he should carry his portion of the world's awful
load. As soon as God opens a man's eyes to behold the appointed
field, may he have the courage to start doing the Father's will,
and the grit to keep on doing it bravely, despite all the critics
on earth and in hell! Then the sheep here at home will not be
scattered abroad without a shepherd.

2. The home pastor should be as *well disciplined as an
army officer.* Sometimes a minister declares, " I do my best
work under pressure." Very well! Apply it from within! At
present we are concerned with parish work rather than personal habits. Nevertheless, a word about them may be in order.
Both in appearance and in dress the servant of God should
keep as neat and clean as any man in uniform. With self-
imposed discipline the minister at home should be as careful as
any lieutenant under the watchful eyes of his captain and colo-
nel. Surely our Lord expects no less of His local representative
than the country requires of an army or navy commander.

The right sort of self-discipline appears in the autobiography of Bishop Edwin H. Hughes, *I Was Made a Minister.*[1] Like
many another clergyman who has become famous, the bishop
started in a small rural parish. There he proved as diligent in
business and fervent in spirit as ever afterward in years of distinguished service. Looking back now, he warns young ministers against " the peril of the extemporaneous." He refers in
part to making ready for the pulpit, but his words also bear on

things pastoral. Whatever a minister does for Christ ought to be carried out with loving care. Only a man's best is good enough for God.

3. The local pastor should be as *skillful as a physician*. If the writer were a man of wealth he would establish a fund for the clinical training of prospective pastors. The course would be given at a general hospital. There the student of pastoral theology would work for six or eight weeks under a Christian physician, as well as a mature nurse. Starting out as an orderly, and then serving as a sort of semimedical intern, he would look at the patient through the eyes of a man with a " healing presence." This line of thought was suggested to the author by a recent experience of six weeks abed in the Presbyterian Hospital at Philadelphia, under the daily care of a physician like the One of Galilee.

A " Summer School for Pastoral Care " is now in operation at Boston. The work is done at the Massachusetts General Hospital, under the auspices of a nonsectarian institute. The course lasts six weeks, and is given twice during the summer. The first two weeks the minister serves as an orderly. " Most of the course deals with actual experiences in ministering pastorally to patients who have been referred to the Protestant chaplain." [2] That sounds admirable. Should there not be such a provision for every seminary student, as well as for parish ministers who desire postgraduate work at a hospital clinic? [3] This movement centers in the hospital where Cabot and Dicks engaged in the work that led to their book, *The Art of Ministering to the Sick.*[4] This volume and two others, out of many, show how the trend has been turning toward things pastoral. The other two are *Highland Shepherds,* by Arthur W. Hewitt,[5] who deals with the rural church, and *The Romance of the Ministry,* by Raymond Calkins,[6] who writes as a city pastor. There have been worthy volumes about the special applications of psychology to our work. These three books have more to do with the routine tasks of the local minister. Is it an accident that all three come from the same part of the country and that no one of them hails from a divinity school? Why do seminaries not assume the leadership in making pastoral theology practical?

4. The parish minister should be as *kind as a saint*. Unfortunately, institutional training often leads to professionalism. Then a person in need becomes only a case, known as " No. 211." What ought to be a heart-to-heart service rendered in the spirit of the Master may degenerate into machinelike " technique." However, well-trained ministers have no monopoly on professionalism. The sorriest blunderbuss may have worked out his own way of doing things wrongly, according to a home-made " technique." Meanwhile, from a Christian physician or surgeon any pastor can learn how to be skillful and kind in dealing with the sick. Fortunately, kindness costs nothing. Often it proves more precious than gold.

In days such as these what do many people need so much as intelligent kindness? Over in Liverpool before World War II the writer ministered for five Sundays at a beautiful church edifice. Out in front stood a monument with the names of the thirty-one sons from the parish who had given their lives during World War I. In succeeding years what did the older folk and the unwedded women of middle age need from their pastor? Kindness and comfort! They wanted him to be a saint of God. They wished him to be gentle, as well as understanding. Such a spirit breathes out from George Eliot's *Scenes of Clerical Life*, a book that every minister ought to read often. These are the closing words:

" There is a simple gravestone in Milby Churchyard, telling that in this spot lie the remains of Edgar Tryan, for two years officiating curate at the Paddiford Chapel-of-Ease, in this parish. It is a meagre memorial, and tells you simply that the man who lies there took upon himself, faithfully, the office of guide and instructor of his fellow men.

" But there is another memorial of Edgar Tryan, which bears a fuller record. It is Janet Dempster, rescued from self-despair, strengthened with divine hopes, and now looking back on years of purity and helpful labor. [She had previously been

a confirmed drunkard.] The man who has left such a memorial
behind him must have been one whose heart beat with true
compassion, and whose lips were moved by fervent faith."

" He hath shewed thee, O man, what is good; and what doth
the Lord require of thee, but to do justly, and to love mercy,
and to walk humbly with thy God? " (Micah 6:8.)

5. The kind shepherd should be as *hopeful as an imprisoned
seer*. Think of the Apostle Paul. From his Roman prison he
wrote the most joyous of his epistles, that to the Philippians. In
Bedford Jail, John Bunyan proved that " stone walls do not a
prison make, nor iron bars a cage." Doubtless both Paul and
Bunyan knew hours of inner gloom. In dealing with other persons, however, each of them kept free from the clutches of
Giant Despair. We too should learn the meaning of " apostolic
optimism," as well as " grace abounding."

At times the pastor may become weary in body, and faint at
heart. He may feel all " cribbed, cabined, and confined." If so,
let him understand that the spirit of the Incarnation leads the
Christian minister to accept limitations gladly for the sake of
doing good. Let him also remember that laymen have troubles
and burdens enough of their own without having to put up
with a petulant pastor. After an unpleasant experience with a
whining parson a good woman spoke about the Pilgrim Fathers: "I thank God for those mighty men, but I praise Him
more for the Pilgrim Mothers. Those heroic women not only
endured all that their husbands had to suffer. The good sisters
likewise put up with the Pilgrim Fathers!"

Looking back we note five marks of the good shepherd.
Someday he will retire, to rest at home beneath the apple tree.
There he will gladly recall the souls he has brought to Christ
and the hearts he has strengthened in God. Such a spirit of
thanksgiving breathes out from a personal letter written to the
author by the late John Kelman, of Scotland. In order to appreciate the message think of him as a good shepherd in days
of war and rebuilding. In 1919 he arrived at New York to assume the pastorate of the large Fifth Avenue Church. He was

far from well, physically. Nevertheless, he started out at once to visit all the members, scattered over the entire metropolitan area.

Later he wrote from his humble cottage home in Edinburgh: " The strain of my two periods of war service, and my experiences in America, proved too much for me. . . . I have had to give up bit by bit the life and work I have loved so well. Now I am retired and on the shelf. . . . That is not so bad a place as it is supposed to be. There is plenty of elbow space, and there are long views. The backward look is fascinating, for my life has been full of interesting experiences. The forward view is rather hazy on this side of the stars. But beyond that is a mysterious and steady light toward which the spirit moves and is full of thanksgiving, as well as peace and joy."

Suggested Readings

Cunningham, William, *The Cure of Souls*. London, 1928.
Kelman, John, *The War and Preaching*. Yale University Press, 1919.

III

The Difficulties of the Work

PASTORAL work may prove more difficult today than ever before. Such service has always taxed a man's time and strength, as well as his brains and perseverance. Although the late Bishop William A. Quayle strongly believed in pulpit work, nevertheless he declared: " Pastoral visiting I deem a greater tax on the faculties than preaching, hard as preaching is. . . . The cure of souls is a severer intellectual task." [1] How would that poetic soul feel if he had to face all the perplexities of the typical parish today, in a world cursed by global war? At times the obstacles seem insurmountable. The clergyman who desires to escape from pastoral drudgery can always find a plausible excuse. Most pastors, however, are sincere in their determination to solve these problems. Why, then, is it difficult to do pastoral work today? Here again, the treatment must be merely suggestive.

1. *The State of the Times.*   At least until recently the trend in our country has been strongly toward secularism.[2] Even within the Church there has been a tendency to lay a veneer of worldliness over things spiritual. At the same time everyday living has become complex. As sons and daughters of Martha we modern church leaders have been busy and troubled about many things. Seldom do we take time to sit down quietly at the Master's feet and learn the one thing needful. In the typical congregation the minister seems to be caught in the contagion of nervous busyness. How can he hope to become holy, as well as happy?

Many of us are beginning to get our bearings. At least we are striving to put the first thing first. That points to the cause of the Kingdom.[3] But we find it hard to rise above the spirit of our age and the habits of our lives. In short, we are typical

28

Americans. In 1930 and again in 1934 some of us visited the Holy Land. Then we journeyed back to Oberammergau. During the second trip, both in Palestine and at the Passion Play, we found that four years had brought increasing " Americanization." By this term one means secularism. Here in the homeland, also, between the Armistice after World War I and the coming of World War II, all of us witnessed a corresponding growth of irreligion. Of late there has been somewhat of a change, but the secular spirit still prevails. Such is the environment in which the clergymen must deal with " modern man in search of a soul."

2. *The Customs of the Home.* Here again, a change for the better seems to have begun. Nevertheless, the pastor must face the decline of religion in many homes of the parish. Only now and again does he learn of grace at meals and of family prayers, of Bible stories at bedtime and of singing hymns while at work, not to speak of the family Bible and religious pictures. All this was to be found in some of the very same family circles a generation ago. As growing boys, many of us could visualize " The Cotter's Saturday Night " long before we first visited bonny old Scotland.

A certain degree of change seems to be inevitable. Because of our mechanized " civilization " all the members of the family circle may not find it easy to sit down together at meals. In fact, the desire to do so may be lacking. How long has it been since you looked in on a fireside group consisting of father, mother, and four or five grown sons and daughters, all sitting together enjoying each other? More likely the older folk have turned on the radio and the younger ones have hied away to the movies. Whatever the reason, the art of conversation seems to have languished. How, then, can the minister expect to do pastoral calling? In an apartment house district, how can he gain access to the habitat of lonely cliff-dwellers?

3. *The Education of the Minister.* The young man may have grown up in a parish where a succession of able clergymen have not had " spare time " enough to know common

people individually. At the divinity school he may have sat under scholars with little show of concern for ordinary folk in sickness and sorrow. In the chapel he may have learned to read impersonal prayers. Is it any wonder that many a seminary graduate thinks of the local church as a preaching station or a business concern? In the pulpit he may attempt to explain certain texts out of the Scriptures, instead of using the Bible to meet human needs.

Does the picture seem overdrawn? If so, think of the special lectures given annually at our best-known seminaries. How often since 1900 has any student of divinity heard a series of scholarly discourses on pastoral theology? In fact, does the typical seminary in the East think it possible to be both scholarly and practical? For instance, who has ever enjoyed a course about " The Good Shepherd in English Literature "? Instead of that, when a distinguished divine feels free to select his subject in practical theology, he addresses prospective pastors on the theme " Six Giants of the American Pulpit." Only one of the six exemplars excelled as a parish minister. On the other hand, who are the heroes of the medical student? Such physicians as the late Richard C. Cabot and Sir William Osler. Neither of them ever became so much concerned about saving the world medically as to ignore the needy patient individually.

We ministers have no monopoly of such shortcomings. They seem to have grown out of American education. The recent annual report of the Rockefeller Foundation presents interesting findings after a study of the physicians now at work in Army training camps. These men have been carefully selected. They prove to be highly skilled in the theory of the medical profession. But there are " not enough doctors capable of handling human beings, capable of understanding the role of emotions and thoughts in disease, capable of listening so wisely to the patient's story of his life and trouble, that diagnosis can be made without large quantities of laboratory tests." [4]

4. *The Outworkings of Original Sin.* In pastoral work the most serious obstacles lie within a man's soul. Whatever the ex-

planation, doctrinally, everyone called to the ministry must battle with the " seven deadly sins." If the reader prefers up-to-date abstract terminology, he can say, " The innumerable, insurmountable obstacles prove to be primarily psychological and subjective." Certain scholars would employ the term " demonic."

A member of our household once asked our neighbor, Dr. Albert Einstein, how he accounted for Adolf Hitler. With a twinkle in his eye the gentlest of scientists answered, " It's all a matter of glands." " Pardon me, sir, but I think it must be the Devil." " Same thing! " said Dr. Einstein with a chuckle. " Same thing! " How far such a line of thought concerns us clergymen, only the Lord can tell. At any rate, we are human and likely to err.

Among the seven deadly sins, pride heads the list. In one of the most helpful treatises about things pastoral, *On the Priesthood,* Chrysostom long ago referred to the minister's chief peril as " self-love." More recently dear old Bishop Quayle declared, " Either a man is too big to make pastoral calls, or he is too little." Whichever it be, the trouble usually springs from pride. According to a wise little book, *Invitation to Pilgrimage,* by John Baillie,[5] pride lies at the root of all our sins. From this tendency to put self in the place of God, who of us can plead exemption?

Neither is a minister immune to covetousness. The typical student of divinity has been forced to economize all his life. After years of self-denial he becomes pastor of a flock that includes a few families with means. Some of them have culture and charm. All unconsciously, they set the social standards for the pastor and his household. Unless he stands on guard, he will defer unduly to these friends and their money. He may even sympathize with the treasurer of a certain church that was struggling to liquidate a huge debt. When the custodian of the Lord's money looked out over twenty-five boys and girls in the pastor's class, he exclaimed: " There's not five dollars in the bunch! " The same sort of mercenary spirit may prevent the

pastor from ministering to all the flock over which God has
made him shepherd.

Is the picture unfair? Perhaps so! Would that it were wholly
untrue! Before you make up your mind, however, confer with
the lay officers of half a dozen local churches. Ask what sort of
demands the up-to-date clergyman makes before he will accept the call to a new parish. Rightly or wrongly, many of our
most spiritual laymen feel that the ministry has become com-
mercialized. Happily, there are all sorts of exceptions.

As for lust, that would warrant a chapter all its own. A few
years ago the writer was asked to address a senior class, infor-
mally, about a young minister's relations with women and
girls. Speaking out of his own experience, the professor told the
young men to be discreet but not unduly alarmed. Within less
than a year he learned that three prominent clergymen, all in
one city, and fairly well known to him, had suffered shipwreck
because of sex. " Wherefore let him that thinketh he standeth
take heed lest he fall." If anyone wishes to follow this trail farther, he can find a wholesome treatment in one of Dr. Richard
C. Cabot's last books, *Christianity and Sex.*[6]

The next three " deadly sins " call for only a passing glance.
Wrath, gluttony, and envy may easily become formidable.
However, they concern a minister's character, whereas the
present discussion relates to pastoral work. If he is a sincere
Christian, he will conquer these demons within his soul.

The last of the seven deadly sins calls for more extended
treatment than we can give at present. Sloth, or laziness, seems
to be the worst of ministerial sins. This evil spirit may brood
over the hours in a man's study. Who but God knows how the
pastor spends his time when alone with books? The same demon may interfere with assiduous toil out in the parish. The
favorite device of this tempter may be procrastination. Repeatedly the demon insists, " Never do today what can be put
off till tomorrow! " That never comes.

Glancing back we note that the chief difficulties in pastoral
work seem as ancient as the false prophets of Old Testament

times. In fact, some of the obstacles go back to Adam. On the other hand, Phillips Brooks insists that a man's ministry, for good or ill, is largely determined by the habits he forms during the first few years after he leaves the divinity halls. Why should he not engage in the right sort of self-discipline while still at the seminary? At least he should learn not to procrastinate.

Let us grant that all kinds of obstacles confront the minister who wishes to become a faithful shepherd. How can he surmount these barriers, without and within? He will find the heart of the matter by reading the spiritual autobiography of the Apostle Paul. In II Corinthians that wise man of God points out the source of the power that makes a man strong and useful:

" My grace is sufficient for thee: for my strength is made perfect in weakness " (ch. 12:9). The familiar lines of Robert Browning also bring cheer. They come near the middle and at the end of " Rabbi Ben Ezra ":

" Let us not always say,
 ' Spite of this flesh to-day
I strove, made head, gained ground upon the whole! '
As the bird wings and sings,
Let us cry, ' All good things
Are ours, nor soul helps flesh more, now, than flesh helps soul! '

     . . .

" So, take and use Thy work;
Amend what flaws may lurk,
What strain o' the stuff, what warpings past the aim!
My times be in Thy hand!
Perfect the cup as planned!
Let age approve of youth, and death complete the same! "

Suggested Readings

McAfee, Cleland B., *Ministerial Practices.* Harper & Brothers, 1928.
Palmer, Albert W., *The Minister's Job.* Willett, Clark & Company, 1937.
Underhill, Francis (ed.), *Feed My Sheep.* Morehouse-Gorham Company, Inc., 1927.

IV

The First Days in a New Field

" WELL begun is half done." In a new pastorate, as in a honey-moon, be sure to make a good beginning. First impressions may be altered, but not easily. Why not start out with traditions of achievement? As the leader in worship and the preacher of the Gospel, why not be at your very best? Never fear that you may afterward fall below such a high level. It is far better to keep reaching up because of previous attainments than to be constantly embarrassed because of past shortcomings.

The chief activities at first should be pastoral. Except for public worship, including the sermon, almost everything else can wait. Concentrate on being a good shepherd. Gain such a reputation, locally. Meanwhile you can be sizing up the situation. Then you can begin making a general plan. In some such fashion Phillips Brooks prepared for his noteworthy pastoral career at Trinity Church in Boston. Starting in at the end of October, 1869, he gave himself chiefly to things pastoral. Gradually he worked out plans for a fruitful ministry during those troublous days after the bloodiest of our wars here at home.

The same principle operates in other fields. As a young man, Booker T. Washington went down to Tuskegee, Alabama, to establish a school for underprivileged Negroes. Arriving in June, he spent the first month out in the community. At the end of that time he seemed to have accomplished nothing tangible. He had simply devoted himself to making friends and to learning facts. When at length he began to lay foundations, he knew exactly what kind of school he wished to build.[1] How, then, should a parish minister start? That depends on what he wishes to accomplish. Let us take for granted that he is spiritually-minded. What should he do first?

1. Let him determine to *know the people in their homes.*
Later it may prove feasible to set apart a " pastor's hour." Then
he can greet his friends, one by one, in the study. But at first
he ought to call in every home. If the new work begins early
in June, he should be able to visit a flock of moderate size before the end of July; if he starts in October, he can get round
before Christmas. Moderate size here means a church with not
more than five hundred resident members. If the minister has
his heart set on something vital which he plans to accomplish
during each call, he can do much in a brief time. How else does
the family physician make his rounds?

After the first visit in a home the minister should have in
hand an accurate list of all the inmates, together with the rele-
vant facts. Ideally, he should inherit such a card index, either
at the church office or else in the study. Actually, not one new
pastor out of a dozen falls heir to an up-to-date list of church
members and adherents. Even so, let him not bewail his fate.
The time and effort spent in ascertaining the facts ought never
to seem wasted. If he forms the habit of praying over each successive name, he can learn how to shepherd the flock by way of
the mercy seat.

Being an effective pastor requires a dependable memory for
names and faces. This faculty seems to be like the imagination,
or any other God-given power, in requiring exercise. The memory gladly serves the man who feeds it with well-digested facts,
and then makes it work. If a minister enjoys reasonably good
health, he can recall whatever he takes the trouble to learn. On
the human level nothing he has gained from books will do
more to insure pastoral effectiveness than the ability to name
all sorts of persons whom he has met only once. Wherein lies
the secret? There seems to be none, at least apart from brains
and work.

The best time to learn a man's name comes at the very first
meeting. Fortunately, the memory for names and faces grows
with use. So does such ability decrease through neglect. Strange
to tell, the more names a minister knows, the more easily can

he learn still another. On the contrary, the parson who contents himself with vague recollections of faces, apart from names, may unconsciously be evading the trouble required to learn accurately. Let him take this as a working motto: " I can recall the name of every person whom I wish to know. By God's grace I shall learn to love everybody." " I can do all things in him that strengtheneth me " (Phil. 4:13).

In Nashville the late Pastor William M. Anderson, Sr., used to enjoy the reputation of knowing every man in town, as well as many of the women and children. Afterward in Dallas he established the same record, but not by accident. He was not born with an uncanny ability to remember names. The dominie never told his lay friends that he associated " Mr. Brown " with the color of his eyes, and " Mrs. Small " with her diminutive stature. In a lecture to theological students, however, this so-called " wizard " opened up his heart.

The visiting divine assured his young friends that he devoted on the average one hour a day to his hobby. Some of us would consider that an extreme. Even so, would it not be wise to set apart an hour a day during the first few months of a new pastorate? How else could the minister and his wife spend an evening more pleasantly than by going over the names of certain new friends in the parish? That was what two of us used to do in each successive congregation. Before we arrived on the field we could tell each other the names of the officers, both the men and the women. When either of us met one of those persons, it was not hard to associate the unknown face with the known name. According to Pastor Anderson, these are " the rules of the game ":

> Be sure to get the name. Spell it distinctly.
> Write it down. Say it aloud, more than once.
> Associate it with something fixed, facially.
> Visualize the other person, with a " camera eye."
> Use the name whenever you meet the person.
> Talk over at night every new name or face.
> Take time. Use all your senses. Will to know.
> Determine by God's grace to excel in this art.

2. The pastor should *win the hearts of all the people.* The best way for a good man to do that is simply to be himself. A minister should school himself to appear friendly. Let him learn how to shake hands. With a man one uses a firm grasp. With a woman one waits until she extends her hand. If she does so, one responds with a degree of restraint. Let the right hand seem neither like a dead fish nor a snapping turtle. Remember that some men like to be slapped on the back, and that others resent such intimacy. The same holds true about the use of the first name. In the words of a wise Episcopal bishop, " If you wish the sexton to address you as ' Mr.,' speak to him as ' Mr.' " Whether or not the minister puts on clerical garb, let the clergyman always act like a clergyman.

In gaining the hearts of the people the main idea is to be concerned about the other person, and then show your interest kindly. Take for granted that the layman wishes to become a better man. Believe in him, and expect much of him as your friend. Erelong you should become his guide and counselor. On the other hand, if any clergyman feigns an interest that he does not feel, sooner or later his sins will find him out. In the practical work of the ministry there can be no substitute for sincere love of people, one by one. The only persons whom the pastor can help are those who like him personally and trust him as a man. In a new field it is easier for them to do so after they have become well acquainted.

3. One ought to *learn the facts about the parish.* After he has mingled with the people for a month or two, a man with open eye and ear can size up the situation locally. Erelong he should know what has been accomplished in recent years. Unless there has been deep-seated dissatisfaction with the preceding regime, the new minister should give much deference to what has been done. In the course of a month or two he should know the field as well as a farmer knows where he should plant his crops and pasture his sheep. After a few more months it may prove necessary to revise the original program. If so, it is relatively easy to change what one has thought out with loving care.

One sort of information should be strictly taboo. Certain officious friends take delight in letting the new leader and his wife know all about the last quarrel in the parish. In such a case let the motto be: " Forgetting the things which are behind, . . . press on." If necessary, one may utter a word of caution: " Please do not tell me that. I wish to be pastor of the whole congregation." Largely because of unwillingness to hear bad tidings from anyone except the culprit concerned, a certain new pastor was able to heal the breaches in a church that had been torn asunder. Years afterward the people still keep saying about him and his wife, " They never knew on which side of the fence any one of us had stood during that awful church fight."

For counsel regarding such delicate matters, go often to Charles H. Spurgeon. In pastoral oversight he was as gifted as in preaching. Once he said to seminary students: " When you commence your ministry make up your mind to begin with a clean slate. Be blind and deaf to the long-standing differences which may survive in the church. . . . Know nothing of parties and cliques, but be the pastor of the whole flock and treat them all alike." [2] In return you will discover that the people rejoice to follow a forward-looking leader.

4. The new minister should gladly *accept parish customs.* Of course he will not countenance anything he knows to be wrong, such as playing " bingo " in a building set apart for the glory of God. Otherwise there can be few exceptions to the following rule: " When in Rome do as the Romans do." The wise young pastor seldom asks for changes in the present way of doing things. If any improvement seems needful, the request will soon come from interested laymen. In his personal habits also, he should conform with the best local ideals and traditions. For instance, look at a recent case.

A new pastor in Jersey City met with difficulty in gaining access to patients whom he was supposed to see at a certain hospital. One day when he had been refused admission he noticed that the Roman priests encountered no such barriers. Not seeing any way out of his dilemma, the pastor went to a more experienced brother. The latter heard the tale and thanked the younger man for coming. Then the older one said: " All you need do is to appear in clerical garb. It will work like a charm." The newcomer did not possess anything of the sort, but he made the needful purchase. Then he found that his difficulties at the hospital largely disappeared.

Would it be wise, therefore, to wear such raiment all the time? That depends on various factors. What an Episcopal clergyman or a Lutheran pastor does as a matter of course might not be wise for a Baptist or a Quaker. As for the writer, he owns clerical attire and dons it whenever that seems to be expected, but not otherwise. Ordinarily, he feels more comfortable without any black raiment. If he had worn a clerical collar in one of his parishes some of his friends might have fainted, or else stomped out of the sanctuary in high dudgeon. Really the whole matter is one of ethical indifference. On the street and in the pulpit the minister ought to wear whatever will help him locally as the servant of God.

The objection to clerical attire seems to be esthetic rather than moral. With all the liturgical colors among which to select, why did the fathers single out black? In olden times the parson used to appear in the pulpit with a widespread white necktie. In full glory he also displayed an expanse of white waistcoat. Of course he wore a stiff white shirt and as high a wing collar as he could endure. All that, happily, has gone out with the passing of the Prince Albert coat and the " stovepipe hat." Nevertheless, on the basis of the New Testament, it would be difficult to justify our custom of garbing the pastor in black. He may wear a gown dark as midnight. If so, why should there not be more than a little of purest white to offset all that appearance of gloom? Candor obliges one to confess that the use of the clerical collar is increasing. If so, perhaps one should conform. At least it still seems proper to lighten the effect by the use of little " tabs " white as the snow on the hills. Some brother should invent bigger tabs!

In short, study the new field, and then plan the work. Begin with your people, not your books. Learn from the apostle: " God is not the author of confusion. . . . Let all things be done decently and in order " (I Cor. 14:33, 40).

Suggested Readings

Brown, Charles R., *The Making of a Minister*. The Century Company, 1927.

Erdman, Charles R., *The Work of the Pastor*. The Westminster Press, 1924.

Gladden, Washington, *The Christian Pastor*. Edinburgh, 1898.

V

The Making of a General Plan

It is difficult to write sensibly about a pastor's program, and still harder to formulate a plan that will work. What suits one minister's personality does not fit another. What proves effective in one parish may fail near by. The way to work in January differs from the ideal method in July. Nevertheless, there is need of a general plan for pastoral work, as well as preaching [1] and other parts of worship.

Being a good pastor ought to become largely a matter of habit. The time to fix the customs for a certain field may be after the first month or two. If one enters the parish at the beginning of June, the best time to draw up the general plan may come during a brief holiday in August; if in October, sometime before New Year's. After two or three months one can look out over the field and see it as a whole. One can formulate a program so as to prevent overlapping of efforts and overlooking of persons. At least that should be the ideal.

From this point of view, a parish minister's life ought to consist of " routine and ideals." That seems to be true even of a poet. Listen to these words about the ablest American bard in recent times: " The man who fixes on something definite in life that he must do, at the expense of everything else, if necessary, has presumably got something that, for him, should be recognized as the Inner Fire. For him that is the Gleam, the Vision, and the Word. He'd better follow it. The greatest adventure he'll ever have on this side will be following where it leads." [2]

Thomas Carlyle sounds even more emphatic: " The longer I live the more am I certain that the great difference between men, between the feeble and the powerful, the great and the insignificant, is energy, invincible determination, — a purpose

41

once fixed, and then death or victory." All the while one ought
to seek and follow the leading of the Spirit, who works according to a plan of His own making.

1. A worthy plan should *include all the people.* The minister's work should allow no room for pets or prejudices. The first
claim on his time and strength comes from the sick and the sorrowing. A sort of priority must also be given to the aged and
the infirm. Much attention should be devoted to newcomers.
All the while the pastor ought to be on the lookout for the
unchurched and the unsaved. His chief concern should be with
the main body of the flock. Is it any wonder that the shepherd
occasionally loses his bearings, and neglects some of the flock?

A plea for " ministerial balance " comes from Bishop Edwin
H. Hughes.[3] He is referring to the regular parish ministry and
not to specialists. This kindly observer of pastors and their
ways reports that World War I led to a lot of unsymmetrical
parish work by zealous parsons. Hence we " well-nigh lost for
the Church one generation of young people." Ofttimes the
ministerial obsession concerned something worthy in itself.
The bishop feels that the parish leaders of today are much
wiser. If so, zeal for the pulpit will not lead to neglect of the
parish, or vice versa. Enthusiasm for Christian world peace,
which every pastor ought to promote, should not cause him to
neglect people who are fighting with fears, if not with each
other.

All this may seem obvious. Perhaps so, but only the exceptional parish leader appears to have made a general plan for his
pastoral work. Why not set down on paper a brief checking
list? Put the substance of it all on a card near the names you
run over almost every week. After next Easter, in reviewing
the past year's work, you may experience a new sense of
achievement. The lay officers will feel gratified because of im-
proved morale among the people. Meanwhile, in more than one
parish the lay officers report that their pastor's methods seem
to be hit-and-miss, with fewer hits than misses.

Look at a concrete case. The congregation numbers approximately five hundred resident members. On behalf of the governing board, one of the officers is speaking to a seminary professor: " We like your former student, both as a preacher and as a man. But unless he changes his habits as a pastor, we shall ask him to leave. He preaches well, especially for a man of his years, and he shows ability as a leader. He appears to be growing in every respect save one: He does not know how to plan his pastoral work. Whenever he goes into a home he wins friends. He likes the people and they enjoy him. But after two years he has not been around our congregation once. Some of our leading members he does not even know. He seems to have been educated under the elective system. Can you help us without hurting his feelings? "

That situation proved easy to remedy. The young man did not realize that he was falling short. Evidently he had not studied William James's well-known essay about " A Certain Blindness in Human Beings." That refers to " the blindness with which we all are affected in regard to the feelings of creatures and people different from ourselves. . . . A pain in him [my neighbor] is not like a pain in me, but something far easier to bear." [4] Fortunately, our religion provides a cure for such a blind spot in the soul.

The professor handled the case indirectly. He went to another minister, and asked him to interview the offending brother. The two were related and were on excellent terms. The pastor in view saw the error of his ways, and determined to reform. The two of them worked out a program for the pastoral oversight of the whole congregation. According to latest reports, the officers are delighted with their " new pastor." So are the rest of the people. Practically all he needed was a workable plan.

If the lay officers had been wise, they would have asked one or two of their tactful men to talk these things over with the minister. Naturally they hesitated to do so. They liked him personally and did not wish to hurt his feelings. Perhaps they also felt that he had not learned to accept such counsel grate-

fully. Even so, they had been elected to represent the people.
In the spirit of Christian love those officers ought to have been
frank with their leader. The possible difficulties in doing so will
appear in the following case. It too concerns an able pastor,
gifted as a preacher. The congregation is larger than in the
preceding case. Otherwise the facts are much the same.

The officers recently instructed one of their number to interview the " pastor." The layman set apart an afternoon and
made an appointment with the minister for an automobile ride
out into the country. When the two men met, the clergyman
began to talk. He knew that the layman earned his livelihood
as a mechanical engineer. Hence the parson proceeded to show
how much he understood about practical mechanics. On and
on the monologue flowed, like Tennyson's brook. After a
while the disheartened layman turned his car round and drove
home. At the first opportunity he reported to the other officers:
" There's no use bothering with such a dunce. A fellow who
will not listen to anybody but himself can never become a
pastor. We must let him go." Soon he was forced to resign.
Then the officials began trying to repair what had gone to
pieces under his unbalanced " leadership."

2. The minister's program should *take account of local ge-
ography*.   The work of planning calls for a map of the community served by the local church. The map requires careful
study until its main features stand out in memory. Then the
pastor can close his eyes and draw an outline of the field, indi-
cating where each family resides. With the map before him as
a guide he can list the households by streets, or by other geographical units, known as districts. He should be able to find
his way over the parish with as much economy of time and effort as a mail carrier or a family physician. Each of those busy
men plans his work.

In Forth Worth, Texas, the pastor of a large congregation
recently told his ministerial brethren about a discovery: " Before gasoline began to be rationed I thought I was conserving
time and strength in my pastoral calling. Now I am covering

the ground as thoroughly as before, with only half the expenditure of gasoline and tires." Meanwhile what occurred? One day he sat down alone to figure out ways and means of covering the parish without waste of energy and time. After he began to work according to a system, he enjoyed pastoral calling still more. So did the people. It pays to plan!

In an Ohio city one of the pastors lives seven miles from a certain hospital. He goes out to that place of healing, on an average, once or twice a week. Starting from his home before two o'clock, he plans to visit eight or ten families who live along one of the various routes to the hospital. The next time he charts a different course and then calls along the way. When it grows too late for visiting in homes where women do their own work, he goes on to the hospital. Of course he would not do so unless he knew that the hour would be acceptable to the superintendent and the nurses.

The customary time for a funeral in that city comes at two o'clock. The nearest cemetery is located four miles from the minister's home. In other cases the distance to the cemetery is longer. Unless the friend in charge of the procession wishes the pastor to ride in a stately equipage, he asks permission to take his own automobile. Fortunately, it looks respectable. After the interment he can make five or six calls directly on the route to his home. Thus he has an excellent reason for not tarrying at the grave after the committal service. However, he must be careful not to appear in a sickroom while garbed as for a funeral. The resulting impression might be depressing!

A recent experience shows that a minister's program must be carried out with discretion. A hospital superintendent vouches for these facts. A lad of twelve years had died after an operation for appendicitis. On the way home from the funeral the clergyman " planned " to visit another boy in that hospital. With growing alarm this lad was facing the same sort of operation. Unfortunately, he knew all about the death of his pal. Coming into the sickroom, with its atmosphere of terror, the clergyman handed over the funeral flowers, explained about the other boy's funeral, and kept on talking mournfully until he had to be sent out of the room. Evidently a system works havoc in the hands of a fool. But he would be as big an ass without any plan. He ought to have chosen to be a butcher.

3. The program should *take account of time.* In a parish of moderate size one may determine to visit every home twice a year. It is almost never wise, however, to make a public announcement concerning the frequency of pastoral calls. The coming of the minister should not seem to be a matter of hard-and-fast routine. As the number of members increases, and other duties multiply, he may not find it feasible to go round the flock more than once a year. Whatever the program with reference to time, he should treat all the people alike. How he does so ought to rest between him and the Lord. Plans are for the pastor, not the people.

The program should lead to intensive visiting during the autumn. Then the weather and the roads keep propitious. A good deal of systematic calling will likewise prove needful after the holidays. However, that period may largely be occupied with the care of the sick and the sorrowing. Disease and death most often abound during February and March. That season also proves fruitful for parish evangelism, culminating at Easter. In other words, the pastor should take account of the changing seasons. Not to do so would indicate a lack of the shepherd heart. The man who works with sheep does not go about his tasks in April as he does in October. Of course any plan must be subject to change, perhaps overnight. Even so, a parish minister accomplishes most for God and men if he works according to a flexible program of his own devising.

Sometimes the parish minister becomes enmeshed in ecclesiastical machinery. At his ordination he promises subjection to his brethren in the Lord. That leads to a vast deal of absence from the home parish. Here is part of a letter from a young minister who is doing a noble work: " Even in North Dakota one of the most sterile activities is attending a multitude of conferences. They seem to be necessary but they consume time out of all proportion to their importance. If we are going to make the Christian Church mighty we must concentrate more on the local parish." The young brother should learn to say no: " I am doing a great work, so that I cannot come down: why should the work cease, whilst I leave it, and come down to you? " (Neh. 6:3).

Such a plan tends to keep the minister at home throughout the year, except during the annual vacation. Five days in the week the pastor devotes to his books and his people. As a rule the morning hours prove most fruitful for study. The evenings may often be given over to meetings. Hence the time for pastoral calling usually comes in the afternoon. One pastor makes it a rule to begin calling two hours after the customary time for starting the noonday meal. In this part of the world lunch begins about twelve o'clock. In South Carolina the main meal of the day used to come at two o'clock, or even three.

The calling should stop at least an hour before the regular time for the evening repast. However harum-scarum the clergyman may be about visiting, housemothers plan their work. If they did not, how could they have time to talk with the pastor? Their program calls for activity before and after every meal. To all these " rules," however, there must be exceptions. In some homes a minister can call at any time.

Prudence likewise forbids a man to enter a certain home that appears on his list for the day. Automobiles parked in front of the house indicate that a feminine group has assembled. If the dear woman is not entertaining her club, she may be engaged in a frenzy of house-cleaning, or fruit-preserving. Again, she may have unexpected guests, who love their pastor back at home.

Under such conditions the woman concerned will appreciate " absent treatment." If the minister draws near, and then decides not to enter the house, he can pass by with a prayer for those whom he has not seen. If he rings the bell before he sizes up the situation, he can simply extend his greetings and promise to call some other day. Fortunately, ministerial tact grows with use. But, alas, so does lack of regard for others. Some of us parsons have a reputation for being ill-bred. Why not follow the Golden Rule?

Is it wise to announce in the bulletin that the minister will call along a certain avenue during the coming week? Ordinarily, no. At a Reformed Church in North Jersey the pastor of a relatively small church has adopted this method, which he commends to his brethren. In a large congregation the plan might not work so well. Are the people along the stated highway to remain at home every afternoon next week? What if unexpected sick calls and funerals keep the pastor from completing his program in five afternoons? On the other hand, if by Wednesday evening he has finished what he started out to do, is he not free to call on some other street? In short, why let pastoral work appear standardized?

A question also arises about the minister's day of rest. In some parishes it seems to become almost hypothetical. At least in theory, a man ought to set apart one whole day in seven for a complete change of thought and feeling. A day of rest, however, need not become a time to rust. Usually a minister takes Monday. Dr. B. C. Clausen, of Cleveland, recommends Tuesday. Henry Ward Beecher used to set apart Friday. An occasional pastor, exceeding bold, insists on Saturday.

The present writer suggests Saturday afternoon and Monday morning. Thus there would come a breathing spell before the most exacting day of the week, with another respite after. Whatever the program, it should be elastic. The needs of men and women ought to take precedence over the convenience of the pastor. For their sake, however, he should strive to reserve a whole day free from ministerial cares and burdens. Only " six days shalt thou labor."

If a man reserves Monday, he may find it hard to take proper care of the sick. For various reasons Saturday and Sunday do not lend themselves ideally to such calls, except in cases of emergency. Often the news about a sick friend comes to the minister on the Lord's Day. If he made the call that afternoon, there might be lay competition. Except in time of crisis, when visitors are not admitted, a sick person may receive too many calls on Sunday afternoon. Why add one more to the number of " Job's comforters "? On the other hand, if one tarries until Tuesday afternoon, one may seem to show little concern. Sick folk tend to be sensitive. So do their loved ones. Hence the writer recommends Monday afternoon for visiting the sick.

Whatever the occasion, a pastoral call should usually be short. In a rural parish the traditions may require a visit, leading up to a sumptuous meal. Such leisurely customs, however, seem to be disappearing. The family physician does not linger in the home an hour or two. Should not the pastor also be busy, and careful about time? Occasionally he finds a situation that leads him to tarry half an hour, or even longer. Normally, he should complete a pastoral call within ten or fifteen minutes. However, there must be no sitting on the edge of the chair, and no signs of a desire to be gone. Relax and listen!

Such a program enables the minister to call at eight or ten homes during an afternoon. This number takes no account of places where the friends are not at home. A man must expect to stop at twice as many homes as he enters. Thus he can cover much ground in five afternoons. Somehow he should gain the reputation that a family physician enjoys: " Our doctor is the busiest man in town. Still he never seems to be in a hurry. No matter how many sick people are waiting for him elsewhere, he always stays until he has done everything he can to make us feel well, strong, and happy." Such a report about the physician of the soul quickly spreads throughout the community. So does the opposite: " Our minister does not like to call. He acts as if he were bored. Why doesn't he stay away? "

If no one is at home, the call need not be wasted. Leave a card showing that you have come. On the reverse side jot down anything you feel led to say, provided it is pleasant, and brief. A near-by pastor uses a double card that folds. On the part exposed to view he has had printed the name of the church, the location, and the hours of public worship. On the lower half of the space appears the name of the minister, with his address, and the time of " the pastor's hour." Since he calls himself " Reverend," which is an adjective, he puts before it that forgotten word " The " and then his full name. It would be more simple to omit the title and identify himself as " John Royal Smith, Minister." Even the Son of Man came to " minister "!

On the inner side of the folded card the two blank spaces afford room for a few words of greeting. Since the pastor must write while standing, the script may loom large. Still he can show concern for the family. Anything personal or intimate would be unwise. No one can tell who may read the message before the friends come home. The next time the minister sees anyone from the household there should be some reference to the intended call. However, there must be no reproach. It cannot constitute an offense for friends to be absent when the pastor comes. His way of appearing should not make them think of the Judgment Day.

4. The program should also *take account of parish organizations.* The wide-awake minister plans to meet the people in groups. He may not belong to the board of trustees, but he can be present fifteen minutes before the time for the monthly meeting. If he likes to be with men, they will enjoy having him present. Some of them will form the habit of coming early to chat with the parson. When the meeting is called to order, he may be invited to lead in prayer. Then he should ask to be excused. If the chairman insists on a word, the pastor may voice the thanks of the congregation for the faithful services rendered by the treasurer and other trustees. Those busy laymen will absorb an astonishing amount of appreciation, when uttered by a minister whom they like and trust.

Much the same kind of opportunity comes often among women. Whenever a " circle " meets, the pastor can be on hand early. Thus he will be ready to hear anything he ought to learn from these busy women. Of course he will not tarry for the program. If two circles convene the same afternoon, from two o'clock until three, he can go to the second group in time for the friendly talk that follows the formal exercises. In such quiet ways he can meet the majority of the active workers almost every month. How could he enlist their support more surely than by showing concern for the cause they love most of all?

If the pastor's engagements permit, he can lead cottage meetings. During the period before Easter, informal gatherings afford an excellent opportunity for neighborhood evangelism. For that line of thought look elsewhere.[5] Here we are concerned with openings for pastoral nurture. However difficult it seems to promote family religion at other times, it should not be hard to strike a spiritual note at a cottage meeting. Fortunate is the congregation whose minister's duties allow him time to prepare for fireside gatherings. Under his leadership the lay friends will enjoy the hour of praise and prayer, with a brief study from the Book. Despite the informality such a meeting calls for careful preparation. Be ready!

All these plans may seem mechanical. So does anything spiritual when you put it on paper. For instance, take the structure of a sermon. As it appears in print the bony framework may look like the skeleton of a horse. But when used aright, the body of the message enables it to move forward as surely as the steed that bore Francis Asbury over his far-flung circuit. On every trip he had in view some destination, clear only to him. Likewise in pastoral work, the program should call no attention to itself. Before a minister has been long on the field, his new friends ought to know that he works as hard as any man in town, and that he accomplishes much in a day, a week, or a year. They should think of their pastor as unhurried, unworried, and unflurried. He knows whither he is bound, and is always on the way.

Does this sound strange in talking about the minister of Christ? [6] In the days of His flesh our Lord worked according to a plan. This truth appears repeatedly in the writings of the late Alexander B. Bruce, New Testament scholar at Glasgow.

While still a parish minister he prepared a volume that has become a classic, *The Training of the Twelve*.[7] There he made clear how our Lord planned His work in the " theological seminary." The same truth bulks large in Bruce's other writings; e.g., *The Galilean Ministry*,[8] and *With Open Face*.[9] In this last-mentioned book appear the following statements regarding " The Synagogue Ministry ": " The plan was a large one "; It showed " a fixed purpose "; " A systematic ministry "; " His beneficent plan "; " A deliberately planned, persistent, extensive effort."

Much the same truth appears in the parables, where our Lord stresses foresight and system, order and industry. He protests against " the life of drift, the half-thought-out " way of doing God's work lackadaisically.[10] From a different point of view this truth emerges in the famous sermon by Horace Bushnell, " Every Man's Life a Plan of God." [11] In a current book that proves thought-provoking, a Canadian divine speaks about our Lord's program: " To read the Gospels is surely to be impressed with the fact that, at least from the beginning of his public ministry, Jesus had a definite conception in mind of what his task was to be." [12] What an example for the parish minister!

Why not plan your pastoral work? But beware not to become the slave of your system. Simply adopt the working philosophy of the Princeton bard:

> " Let me but do my work from day to day, . . .
>   Let me but find it in my heart to say,
>   When vagrant wishes beckon me astray,
>   ' This is my work; my blessing, not my doom;
>   ' Of all who live, I am the one by whom
>   ' This work can best be done in the right way.'
>
> " Then shall I see it not too great, nor small,
>   To suit my spirit and to prove my powers;
>   Then shall I cheerful greet the labouring hours,
>   And cheerful turn, when the long shadows fall
>   At eventide, to play and love and rest,
>   Because I know for me my work is best." [13]

Suggested Readings

Beaven, Albert W., *Putting the Church on a Full Time Basis*. Doubleday, Doran & Company, Inc., 1928.

Beaven, A. W., *The Local Church*. Abingdon-Cokesbury Press, 1937.

Fenn, Don Frank, *Parish Administration*. Morehouse-Gorham Company, Inc., 1938.

Leach, William H., *Church Administration*. George H. Doran Company, 1928.

VI

The Place of the Pastor's Wife

THUS far we have said practically nothing about the minister's wife. Of course she ought to be a sincere Christian, and a believer in his work as a pastor. If she proves worthy of her calling as his partner, she can almost double his usefulness. If she falls short — through lack of piety, ability, or charm — she may drive him into life insurance work. In short, like her husband, she ought to be called of God, and feel highly honored.

In some respects her province resembles that of the physician's wife. Each of them can render a noble service by making the home life comfortable and happy, as well as by keeping her husband free from domestic cares. The demands on the minister's wife, however, prove far more exacting. Only by the grace of God can she show herself worthy. By His blessing she can become " a friend at large." She can learn to love everybody, and then everybody will love her. In her life and work, love for God and people will insure the fulfilling of every law.

1. *The Wisdom of Working Indirectly.* In some fields the policy here advocated may not prove feasible. With certain women the call of duty may lead otherwise. As a rule the pastor's wife can do most good indirectly. If she accepted the responsibility for leading the choir, the missionary society, or any other cross section of the local church, she might become overburdened, so as to neglect her husband and children. Even if she had the time and strength, she might incur criticism. Probably she can do more good by encouraging others to lead. Every society ought to have in the ranks some person with charm and tact who always cheers the leader.

Should the wife accompany the minister on his calls? As a rule, no. When she first appears as a bride she will go with him until she feels at home. Soon she may discover that these calls

54

become social, not religious. Only occasionally can two persons receive the sort of confidences that the minister expects when alone. That may be why the family physician does not take his wife when he visits the sick.

Unless the pastor helps with the housework, his wife cannot accompany him every afternoon. If she visits some families and not others, she may be accused of playing favorites. If there are children in the manse, she cannot spend five afternoons elsewhere. If there are no little ones as yet, it is scarcely wise to start what she cannot keep up. Whenever she has time for calling, she can go out alone to take care of special cases — shut-in friends, it may be, or those in sorrow. There is always something useful for the pastor's wife to do. In fact, unless she is careful, she may attempt too much.

In time she ought to become known among women and girls as a personal counselor. To her the pastor may send a woman or girl in need of such intimate counsel as he can scarcely give. To make that suggestion, however, calls for ministerial tact. What many a tempted or erring sister really needs is the loving-kindness of a good woman who knows how to listen without feeling shocked. Only a minister's wife can tell how many women and girls go about with broken hearts. Why should there not be in the parsonage a loving friend who will guide such a seeker into the pathway of peace?

The most immediate privilege of the pastor's wife is to make her husband happy. The best place to let her light shine is through the windows of a happy home. She can help her beloved in countless ways: by being cheerful, at least when he is at home; by making the house neat and attractive; by planning wholesome meals, not too heavy; by promoting nonparochial talk at the table; by keeping him from overindulgence of appetites; by rearing several children aright; by talking over any problem on which he wants light; and by refraining from being the " boss " of the congregation. She may be the power behind the throne, but she ought not to wield a big stick. Love works best by indirection.

If such a statement sounds exacting, the reason may be personal. At recent conferences of ministers the writer has held a good many interviews with bewildered pastors. Most of them have wished counsel regarding their wives. Doubtless there was another side to each story. Even so, the happiest and the most useful ministers in each assembly were those whose wives made home seem like heaven. At present we are concerned with what a good woman can do for God indirectly, by helping her husband become a radiant pastor.

What should she do about his sermons? She can aid him far more by intelligent praise than by rigorous criticism. She ought to deal with his pulpit work as she wishes him to do with her cooking: regard it all with the eyes of love. If she is doing her best, so is he. Instead of sitting in " the seat of the scornful," let her find a place in the cheering section. Of course she will soon begin to notice annoying mannerisms of which he is not aware. She will wonder at his original way of pronouncing certain words. She may feel like protesting when he lets his voice soar higher and higher, all the while becoming more nasal. Does she not believe in the holiness of beauty? Even so, let her wait and pray.

One of the worst things a pastor's wife can do is to find fault with his preaching before he has regained his equilibrium. He may feel wretched enough without having a shower of cold water administered by one whom he loves. In short, let there be no wifely faultfinding on the Lord's Day. Surely there must be something to commend, if it is only a luminous text. Later in the week she can tell him, tactfully, anything that still seems needful. But let it be in love, and gently. Has she not taken him " for better for worse "? What could be worse than some of his sermons, and better than much of his pastoral care? If she became a nagging critic of his pulpit work, she might make him a self-conscious weakling.

When the pathway of wifely duty seems hazy, she ought to have at hand a " mother confessor " who can serve as a very present help in time of need. In some other parsonage not distant, the young mistress of the manse ought to find a motherly friend who will gladly serve as comforter and guide. From her the younger woman can learn how to excel in the most difficult work God commits to any of His daughters: that of being at the same time a loving wife and a minister's partner. Gradually she can learn how to live with him in a house by the side of the road and be a friend of everybody. In time she ought to become known as the most winsome woman in all her world.

The woman of God's own choosing needs what Sir James M. Barrie calls charm. In his domestic drama, *What Every Woman Knows,* charm is said to be " a sort of bloom on a woman. If you have it, you don't need to have anything else, and if you don't have it, it doesn't matter much what else you have." The young woman's charm will be sure to increase if she keeps on being educated aright. Otherwise she may become only a household drudge, unable to live on the level with her husband as he grows in wisdom and spiritual stature. Why, then, do we almost never pray for the mistress of the manse?

2. The Choice of a Special Niche. After the first six months in a field, the pastor's wife can surely discover some need that is not being met. If so, this may be the special niche God has appointed for her. Instead of interfering with the work of any existing society, she can render a beautiful service distinctively her own. If so, she must not lessen her concern for the regular work being done by the women of the parish. If they have learned to love and trust her, they will be glad to let her do whatever her heart directs.

In three different parishes the author's wife found a need for special work among business women and girls. In each case she led them to form a group for Bible study. They also met for social enjoyment and the promotion of social service in the community. In one group a number of the " girls " had been divorced through no fault of their own. Others had trials and problems that tended to fade away after the group began to bring peace into aching hearts. The " girls " themselves filled the offices and did the larger portion of the work. The minis-

ter's wife led them in reading together a chosen book of the
Bible, such as St. Luke, or The Acts, and in applying Biblical
truth to all sorts of human needs.

A still more essential kind of service will appear in the chapter about " The Enlisting of Lay Visitors." The idea is for the
pastor's wife to lead other women in calling that might otherwise be neglected. There must be no appearance of devising
something novel to keep them busy as mere gadabouts. Neither must there be any assumption of authority. The wife of a
beloved pastor is subject to all sorts of scrutiny. Woe be to her
if she seems to be trying to manage the congregation. On the
other hand, by sweetness and gentleness she can help her husband to avert all sorts of parish tangles. Most of them start
among women who have not enough work to keep them out of
mischief.

3. *The Location of the Parsonage.*   Where should the two
parish leaders reside? As a rule they ought to live in the house
set apart by the congregation. Not to do so might seem snob-
bish. Except for the church edifice, no building in the community should exert a more beautiful influence. Round these two
foci, the church and the manse, the spiritual and social life of
the parish ought to revolve. Where, then, should the church
fathers erect the parsonage? (We who are Scottish term it the
manse!) The usual alternatives are three:

Often the pastor lives next door to the church. That may
be convenient for him, but it is hard on his wife. Her household regime may be subject to constant oversight. Her children
will receive undue attention, if not teasing. They may not have
a sunny place to play outdoors. Her pots and pans will be borrowed and returned half-burned. Her personal life may become submerged in parish concerns. She may have to entertain
bores by the hour, and drive away book agents with the broom.
Before long she will know why the physician's wife prefers to
live at a distance from his office.

An occasional city pastor can afford to reside out in the suburbs. Six days in the week he must commute. In a downtown

church, surrounded by skyscrapers, such a remote domicile may seem inevitable. It affords advantages the reverse of the drawbacks mentioned above. Theoretically, the husband can pack up all his troubles and leave them downtown. The wife can have a flower garden, and call her soul her own. The children can enjoy sunshine, fresh air, and freedom from fools who kiss little girls on the cheek and pat little boys on the head.

On the other hand, when the pastor's wife dwells up on the mountain it is hard for her to do much work down in the valley. How can she identify herself actively with people among whom she does not reside? Is she to become a commuter? Are the children to see the home church only on Sunday? It must be difficult even for her husband to do his parish work partly by " remote control." With certain exceptions, the pastor and his wife should dwell near the church.

If the average minister and his family had their way they might vote for the third plan. It calls for a comfortable parsonage, not hard to heat, two or three squares from the church, or at least within walking distance for both husband and wife. Thus the pastor and his family can enjoy a home life of their own. All the while they can live so close to the center of the congregation that they can almost hear every heartbeat. Is not such a choice in keeping with the spirit of the Incarnation? In fact, any needful sacrifice may be somewhat like that of the Cross. For instance, look at an actual case.

Years ago the late George F. Pentecost was called to the pastorate of our Bethany Church in Philadelphia. Since the church was situated in " the poorer part " of the city, the lay officers supposed that he and his wife would live out in the suburbs. However, the laymen deferred to his request for a humble dwelling down among the people. There in a tiny domicile, as spotless as snow on the mountains, the writer once called, after the minister had gone home to his God. The assistant pastor lovingly showed the guest a picture of Dr. Pentecost's summer home in Connecticut. To the young visitor that mansion up in the hills looked like a castle fit for a king. Ever since then the

writer has understood more clearly " the grace of our Lord
Jesus Christ ": " Though he was rich, yet for your sakes he
became poor, that ye through his poverty might become rich "
(II Cor. 8:9).

All this concerns the minister's wife acutely. The setting of
the home means more to her than to him. If she were not willing to make such a sacrifice, she would not be worthy to become the wife of a pastor. However unlovely the surroundings,
she can do most good by living among the people, as one of
them. Thus she can afford every growing girl an example of
queenly grace. She can set before every growing boy a pattern
of womanly charm — unlike, it may be, that of his mother. As
the pastor's wife mingles with the people, she can show them
how to be friendly without becoming effusive, and how to love
God without losing the common touch.

Is it any wonder that many a strong parish minister says, sincerely: " Under God, I owe everything to my wife "? In our
own congregation the leading soprano said one day: " Our pastor must have a beautiful home life. Whenever he mentions
household religion, as he often does, he looks radiant. With
such a wife, is it any wonder he always seems happy? "

Suggested Readings

Bader, Mrs. Jesse M. (ed.), *I Married a Minister*. Abingdon-Cokesbury Press, 1942.
Hewitt, Arthur W., *The Shepherdess*. Willett, Clark & Company,
   1944.
Johnson, Mrs. Anna F., *The Making of a Minister's Wife*. D. Apple-
   ton-Century Company, Inc., 1939.

VII

The Call in a Typical Home

THE man with the shepherd heart enjoys making pastoral calls. Since he loves the Lord and cares for people, he believes in them and in household visitation. He discovers that he does not really know the people until he has seen them in their homes. Even if calling were not a God-given means of nurture for the laymen concerned, it would prove beneficial to the pastor.

Despite the importance of these contacts, if you ask an effective pastor how to make a call, he can scarcely tell. The answers vary according to the personality of the minister, the prevailing climate of the home, the season of the year, and other factors hard to define. Whatever the reason, scarcely any two calls prove to be the same. Herein lies the difficulty of the work, and much of the fascination. How then begin?

1. *The Habit of Making Ready.* Before the pastor starts on the afternoon round, he should make up a calling list. If he studies at the church — as he probably should, if only for the sake of his wife — he makes his preparations there, before he goes home for lunch. He takes out of the " district files " the cards for twice as many families as he expects to visit. These cards he arranges in the order of the calls, geographically. Then he puts the cards in the thin notebook that he carries in the left side pocket. On each card he finds written the names of the friends in the home, and any other facts he should recall.

These cards he does not show to any layman. The hieroglyphics on the back might arouse curiosity. One minister used at times the letters, " C.P.," by which he meant " Cold Parlor." As a rule a man finds a note giving the date of the last call, and perhaps the number of the psalm that he read. In making such entries the pastor resembles a wise physician, who records everything that will help the next time he enters the home.

61

Especially is it important to know the names of the children, and the facts about the sailor lad overseas.

Even after these preliminaries it may prove hard to fare forth each afternoon. When two o'clock draws near, one may be deep in a book of theology or verse. One may feel tempted to wait for the afternoon mail. Even so, if one sallies out on time, one soon begins to feel refreshed. Unless one encounters cases that almost break the heart, one may come home whistling. With all due regard for Emily Post, a minister can do much worse at home than whistle. In short, any man who loves to make calls can learn how. Keep right with God, and then let your heart have its way.

2. *The Way to Enter a Home.* Draw near to each home in the spirit of prayer. While waiting for someone to respond, after you ring the bell, ask the Lord to bless each member of the household. Seek His guidance and restraint in all that is said and done. If no one happens to be at home, still God is waiting to answer " the effectual fervent prayer of a righteous man." The one now standing at the door looks on the Christian family as the most vital institution on earth. Ideally, he thinks in terms of heaven. Actually, he knows how it savors much of earth. Spiritually, he expects to see it transformed.

Outwardly, at least, the minister acts as if he were making a social call. However, if he finds people at home, he does not leave a card. Unless the weather is cold or inclement, he removes his hat before anyone opens the door. If he is wearing overshoes he removes them, as well as the topcoat. The rubbers he leaves outside; the umbrella he puts where the hostess indicates. So he does with hat and overcoat. Not every person he visits will expect such courtesies, but still he ought to keep in practice. In short, let him act like a gentleman.

In the room he sits down, but not while his hostess remains standing. All the while he should look happy. Thus he gives the impression that this home should be the house of God and the gateway of heaven. As for the conversation, there can be only a few suggestions. One is to talk deliberately. Then he is more

likely to be interrupted. Another is to listen more than he
speaks — during all but the last few minutes. Near the close
of the time allotted, the minister takes charge of the conversation, tactfully. Thus the end should crown the call.

The clergyman finds that people vary widely. In terms that
leave much to be desired, some of them are introverts; others,
extroverts. Among the former, who may not be numerous, the
pastor is obliged to do practically all the talking. That may not
be according to his ideals, but how can he change human nature? For this kind of experience he ought to be prepared. If
he has made his heart ready for the afternoon's work he may
lead taciturn friends close to God. A case from life will show
what sometimes occurs.

The elderly father and mother were of the stolid type. He
had retired from business. Except for the servants, the two
lived alone in a mansion. Both thought continually about their
son up in the mountains, battling with tuberculosis of the
lungs. In that home every few weeks the minister felt obliged
to " take charge of the service." The first few times he shrank
from passing over the threshold. After a while he discovered
that those elderly folk loved their new pastor. Now he feels
certain that his calls were dearly prized and that they did lasting good. Still waters often run deep. God's dearest children
may not be known for their much speaking.

At the next home the friends were of the effervescent sort.
Here the pastor enjoyed every minute, though in later years he
wondered whether or not he accomplished anything lasting. At
any rate, the mother had been wanting to see the minister.
The father seemed to be bursting with the desire to tell about
the exploits of the son beyond the sea. The two parents talked
at once. Gradually the caller tried to direct the stream of talk
into a channel that would suggest a passage from the Book and
a word of prayer. Meanwhile he listened. Except near the close
of his stay, he kept on the receiving end of the line. Even so, he
went away with a feeling of futility.

3. *The Spirit of the Call.* The spirit of the " born pastor "

differs from that of the pulpit orator. Ofttimes one who excels
in household visitation does so partly because of an unassertive
personality. Where the other minister would thrust himself
into the center of the stage and dominate the scene, the man
with the shepherd heart prefers to listen. This he does eagerly.
Where the other would leave an impression of his commanding
presence, the self-effacing pastor seems intent on learning about
the friends in the home. To him they open up their hearts and
pour out their troubles.

Sometimes the pastor takes himself too seriously. As Queen
Victoria used to say about Mr. Gladstone, " He speaks to me as
if I was a public meeting." When a young man goes courting he
may figure out a psychological approach, only to discover that
the beloved made up her mind before he began to speak his set
piece. In pastoral work, one takes for granted the sincerity of
the welcome. As friend meets with friend, there should be no
ice to break, at least for the minister. Soon the word goes round
that the new pastor knows how to listen. He likes to call, and
the people enjoy having him come.

Usually the minister goes by himself. Occasionally the writer
took with him a spiritually-minded officer of the home church.
One afternoon the layman was a popular professor at the university. For reasons of his own he insisted on taking only a minor part in the proceedings. When the two friends parted the
layman thanked his pastor for the privilege, and then added:
" I never knew that calling was so enjoyable, and so hard to do
well. In each of the eight homes you made a different approach,
and guided the conversation into a different channel. Pastoral
visiting must require even more brains than preaching." Amen!

4. The Course of the Conversation. The friendly talk
moves round two foci: the present home and the near-by
church. Of the two, the home comes first. That is where the
friends are at the moment. If there are children they soon enter the picture, close to Christ at the center. Erelong the conversation shifts to the eldest son, across the sea and exposed to
peril. After the home has had its due, the talk shifts to the

1. home
2. Church

congregation. If the father or mother serves as a leader, the pastor shows how much he cares for that part of the church life.

Gradually the minister can introduce whatever lies closest to his heart. In every round of calls there ought to be some cause that he wishes to present. He may be striving to foster good will toward the Japanese and the Germans, against whom we unwillingly went to war. If the affairs of the household seem tangled, he may have no opportunity to broach the wider subject. Even so, he cherishes the ideal of promoting world brotherhood by teaching the friends in each home to love our enemies beyond the seas.

Other causes may enter the conversation. As a rule there should be only one during a given call. The choice depends on the season, and the spiritual state of the parish. The talk may turn to evangelism, the use of the Bible in the home, or the Christian nurture of children. Strange to say, many a zealous mother does not know how to tell Bible stories, or where to find them in books. Neither does the father know how to conduct family prayers. Such friends need personal counseling more than pulpit exhortation. Facts help them more than theories.

This kind of calling requires courage. Often it would seem easier to talk about the weather. If that appears to be the only topic available, use it for the glory of God. According to Gipsy Smith, Sr., " The Lord's weather never interferes with the Lord's work." Once in Columbus, Ohio, Dr. Robert E. Speer preached at a church where he was highly revered as a statesman in the Kingdom. That morning the rain fell in torrents. When the pastor expressed his regrets, almost apologetically, Dr. Speer replied that he felt no such concern. " When the people put much into churchgoing they receive all the more. We are sure to have a royal time in the House of the Lord today." So we did!

Pastoral calling affords an opportunity to encourage churchgoing as a habit. If this be the theme, there should be no semblance of gloom. Rather let the talk seem sprightly. The same principle holds true about giving. If the pastor is wise, he leaves to the laymen all soliciting of funds. But when a friend in perplexity inquires about giving, the minister can make clear the ideals of the New Testament.

In the course of a week the pastor can help to solve many problems relating to church or home. Whatever the subject, he ought to speak with " apostolic optimism." Better still, he should listen with patience, much like that of God with our faltering prayers.

" What if the friends keep talking about their garden? " Is there nothing in the Scriptures about seedtime and harvest? Does not the Book tell about preparing the soil and tilling the ground? With no more sermonizing than people expect from a parson, lead the conversation around to the fact that in the spiritual life of home and church results follow causes. If the minister loves the Lord and knows the Bible, he can lead Victory gardeners to look on their everyday avocation in terms of God and the Kingdom.[1]

That may be the ideal. What are the facts? Alas, the conversation may keep on being secular. That may be God's way of helping pastor and people to know each other. Sometime sorrow may strike that household. Then he will come as a friend. If the minister bears about a " healing presence," his visits will make God seem close and heaven dear. Especially should the spiritual note prevail during the last few minutes of a pastoral call.

5. *The End of the Call.* It may prove hard to leave. If so, as in a sermon, the reason may be that one has no clear aim. Before he makes ready to depart, the pastor may inquire: " Is there anything special about which you wish me to pray? " The answer may bring out what he has in mind. Even so, the fact that the request comes from the other person should insure a co-operative prayer.

In short, enter the home as a friend. Tarry ten or fifteen minutes. Keep the windows of the soul wide open to sense

what is needed most. Serve these friends as their spiritual physician. When you leave, do so as the pastor of the entire family,
including the absent ones. They are far away from home, but
ever near to God. During the call, gradually there should be
a shifting of emphasis from the viewpoint of a friend to that
of a physician and then that of a pastor. Fortunately, all three
can be aspects of one loving personality. Whatever the need,
the Holy Spirit stands ready to guide. Reverently one may para-
phrase an old-time hymn: " Holy Spirit, faithful Guide, ever
near the pastor's side." Really the Spirit abides in the shepherd's
heart, and leads him by an inner light.

In coming chapters we shall deal with special problems.
Here we think of the normal home, which presents few difficulties. The conversation begins with the people where they
are, as personal friends. It closes with the blessing of the Triune
God. The home and the church dominate the scene. Under God,
the welfare of this family depends largely on means of grace
that center in the sanctuary. Even more the well-being of the
congregation depends on the spiritual health of the various
homes. Thus the call should bind home and church together in
the service of God. Then home and church will work together
for the extension of the Kingdom throughout the world.

6. *The Things to Avoid.* Some of the following counsels
ought to prove needless. Unfortunately, they grow out of recent cases, which may be far from typical. No gentleman
would " park " his chewing gum or cigar on the front porch.
If anything of that sort seems needful, it belongs at home.
Why, then, did that woman tell a group of friends how she
had to keep her pastor from smoking in her house? In a book
that searches the conscience,[2] Dr. Nolan B. Harmon, Jr., tells
of a father who asked his minister not to smoke in the presence of the growing boys in that family. They looked up to the
pastor as their hero. For their sake the clergyman stopped using the weed. If a man must smoke, he need not do so in public. Some good people resent that sort of pastoral burnt offerings.

Within the house there need be no mud on the shoes. If
some persists in clinging, one does not wipe it on an Oriental
rug, or even on Brussels carpet. That is not the approved
method of cleaning shoes. It may prove necessary to tarry in
the living room while little Mary informs her mother about the
guest downstairs. If so, do not " improve the shining moments " by roaming around peering at pictures and dipping
into books. They may need dusting. Sit down and remain
seated until the heart of the household appears in person. Then
rise and greet her without a sense of shame because of pastoral
curiosity. " When I became a man, I put away childish things."

Do not show consciousness of passing time. Do not sit on
the edge of the chair and look at the clock on the mantel, or
keep glancing at the wrist watch. That was not why the friends
gave their pastor a handsome present. In one of her novels
about life in Virginia, Ellen Glasgow makes a certain character say that the doctor and the nurse have fallen into the habit
of looking at the wrist watch. If the minister does so, the
friends may wish that he had not come, for he seems anxious
to depart. Without lolling about as though there were nothing
more to do all day, he can call deliberately and yet leave soon.
Be not a " timeserving pastor."

Do not ask to see little boys and girls. If they are at hand, as
well as presentable, the mother will produce them proudly.
Then you will need to employ all your tact and charm. Other-
wise, why cause embarrassment to her and annoyance to them?
They do not wish to quit their games. If they come in, thank
God. If they do not, inquire about them, one by one. Remem-
ber each of them, preferably by name, in the closing prayer.
No matter how much the minister loves to see boys and girls,
he should ask himself if he liked to be dragged into the " par-
lor " years ago and patted on the head or kissed on the cheek.
Such things went out of style with the white necktie and the
Prince Albert coat.

As a rule do not take notes while in view of the friends. At
the first call it is proper to jot down the facts about the fam-

ily. After that, do not act like a census taker, or a representative of the Gallup Poll. Give the impression that you are deeply interested, and that you will remember everything you learn. If you promise to write a letter, however, or look up a stranger, jot down the data at once in the vest pocket engagement book. Writing out such facts will aid the memory.

Do not feel disheartened if a call appears fruitless. Even the noblest saints cannot dwell continually on the mountaintop. If a family seems below par spiritually, the pastor's coming ought to prove timely. His presence should work like a tonic. Is he not the bearer of good news from God? Yea, verily, but the virtue goes out of the man who guides conversation through surrounding gloom worse than fog in a mountain dale. After such an experience the pastor may feel that he has accomplished nothing. How can he know? Only God can read hearts that are cast down. He can bless the appointed means of grace. Trust Him! No one can tell which calls have done good, or, it may be, harm.

These negations suggest other faults, perhaps worse. For instance, a clergyman may tell shocking jokes. Such lapses may be due to lack of culture. Often they come from carelessness. A tactless person seldom knows how many toes he has trampled during an afternoon when he imagines he has done good. A prominent layman said recently about his pastor emeritus: "If we could have kept the old doctor in the study and the pulpit, he would not have made our people mad. But when he got out of his orbit he offended our friends right and left. They felt prompted to pray, 'From that kind of pastoral visitation the good Lord deliver us!'"

Such blunderbusses seem to be rare of late. The standards of ministerial manners have been rising ever since some of us were young. On the stage the Protestant clergyman occasionally appears as a caricature, but he represents days bygone. With few exceptions the pastors whom the writer knows well seem to be like "The Parson" in *The Canterbury Tales*, by Geoffrey Chaucer:

" Wide was his parish, scattered far asunder;
Yet none did he neglect, in rain or thunder.
Sorrow and sickness won his kindly care;
With staff in hand he journeyed everywhere.
This good example to his sheep he brought,
That first he wrought, and afterwards he taught. . . .

" To draw his flock to heaven with noble heart
By good example was his holy art.
Nor less did he rebuke the obstinate,
Whether they were of high or low estate.
For pomp and worldly show he did not care;
No morbid conscience made his rule severe.
The lore of Christ and His apostles twelve
He taught, but first he followed it himself."

Such a spirit of love and concern likewise dominates the calling of city pastors. Think of Dr. George A. Buttrick among the many people of the Madison Avenue Church in New York. The young men from his congregation report that he has a unique way of closing a call. After a word from the Book, and a brief prayer, he says in substance, just before he departs: " Tonight at ten o'clock in my home I shall be praying for you friends by name. At the same hour I wish you to be praying for me, and for the church that we all love." Thus the pastor and his friends often meet around one common mercy seat.

Suggested Readings

Adams, Hampton, *The Pastoral Ministry*. Abingdon-Cokesbury Press, 1932.
Pleune, Peter H., *Some to Be Pastors*. Abingdon-Cokesbury Press, 1943.

VIII

The Wisdom of Offering Prayer

Is it wise to offer prayer at the end of every call? Perhaps not, but the exceptions prove to be *very* few. After twenty-six years in the pastorate, a well-known clergyman declared that he could remember only once when he had erred in offering to pray. For seventeen happy years the present writer served as a parish minister. He made it a rule to pray in each home, but he did not enforce the rule with an iron hand. He too can recall only one instance when he should not have led in prayer. On the other hand, he waived the rule too often. What a coward!

1. The Desire to Offer Prayer. Before embarking on his lifework as a pastor, the clergyman should make up his mind about the efficacy of prayer. Is it a means of grace in the home, as well as the sanctuary? Can there be any substitute for the right sort of prayer at the end of a normal call? If not, he should make ready day by day. There can be little benefit from the kind of talk that costs nothing. If prayer is " a battlefield," the leader ought to be ready for action, and for victory. Before entering the home, decide about the aim of the closing prayer. If conditions call for something different, the heart will be ready to intercede about that. In short, " pray without ceasing."

Encourage the people to expect a prayer. At the beginning of the pastorate foster such a feeling. In the bulletin, and at times verbally, make some such request: " When the pastor comes into your home, invite him to read a passage and offer prayer." Thus the most timid clergyman can set up for himself and his friends a spiritual ideal. Whenever he crosses the threshold of a house, he should enter as the shepherd of souls. Without saying so to anyone else, he may resolve: " By God's grace, I shall never be asked to pray in a home with sickness or sor-

[margin notes: An experience of worship in the home / Worship with the Family]

71

row where I have not first prayed in a time of sunshine and peace." That sort of pastor soon becomes known as " a man of God."

Why should any such notice prove necessary? Whatever the reason, facts are facts. In the " new " pastorate the friends may have become accustomed to a minister who prayed. If so, they should thank God for another man of His own choosing. On the other hand, cases such as the following are not uncommon. A Presbyterian elder was stricken with paralysis. After eight more years in the parish where he had served diligently, he went with his family into the bounds of another congregation. Soon the " new " minister called, and led in prayer. Later the wife told him: " Except for my own feeble words, that was the only prayer my husband has heard in eight years." " Did not his pastor call? " " Yes, but he told jokes." " Why didn't you invite him to pray? " " I didn't know that was proper any more. Anyhow, he didn't act like a praying man."

In another community a certain husband belonged to one congregation and his wife to another. That may never be ideal, but in the case before us the arrangement appeared to work well. In course of time the middle-aged husband suffered a stroke. He had been a deacon in the church, which he dearly loved. Every few weeks his pastor called. So did the wife's minister, though less frequently. Both of them tried to bring sunshine in the way of innocent humor, as the invalid seemed likely to live for years. At the end of a call the wife's minister always assumed the privilege of reading from the Book and offering prayer. One day the wife followed him out to thank him for such thoughtfulness. Then she said much the same as the woman quoted above. Neither of them had dared to suggest that the " man of God " stop being " funny " long enough to deal with religion. All the while that came first in the heart of the stricken layman.

2. *The Exceptions to the Rule.*   In either of these cases any spiritually-minded clergyman would pray. In other calls, however, the path of duty may not seem clear. For instance, when

young and callow the writer once went into a home where the people were strangers. They had not invited him to call, but they treated him courteously. He discovered that they were devoted members of the Catholic Church near by. Before he departed he asked the privilege of leading in prayer. Now he knows that he blundered.

If such circumstances seem exceptional, that is the point. Do not feel obliged to pray under the wrong conditions. Consider another case: A minister in quest of stray sheep was asked to call at the home of certain newcomers. Early in the visit, which proved enjoyable, he discovered that they were devout Baptists. He promised to get in touch with the local Baptist minister immediately. Just as the first man of God was making ready to leave, with something close to an apology, in came the Baptist pastor. Fortunately, the two clergymen liked each other. Neither suspected his brother of stealing sheep. Even so, that was one case in which the first man showed wisdom in not offering to pray. He did not wish to " win friends and influence people " in a Baptist household.

In circumstances much more common, the minister finds the people sitting on the front porch. There they visit with him for a while. He is not ashamed to be seen praying in view of the neighbors. But he knows that the friends in this home feel sensitive about such things. They do not wish to parade their piety, about which they may be dubious. He should sympathize with this feeling, which they would not express. Ordinarily, he should not close such a call with prayer. If there were a special reason for his doing so, he would ask them to go inside. There they could offer up sacrifices to God without being seen of men. All the while the rule should hold: If feasible, pray in every home, and do so at the end of every call.

3. The Way to Offer Prayer.   Again we face that perplexing word, How? Who can tell? Every minister ought to approach the mercy seat in a manner all his own. In each household one ought to pray according to the climate that prevails. Even so, a few suggestions may prove helpful. First of all, let the prayer be short. It should concern the spiritual interests of this home, and little else. There may be a few words about the local church. So should there be petitions for our land in her time of distress, and for a world that has been at war. These parts of the prayer, however, should spring out of what concerns this home. In short, begin with the friends where they are, and lead them close to the heart of God.

The form and the content of the prayer should differ somewhat from day to day and from house to house. Otherwise a man might fall into formalism, and begin talking like a parrot. If he knows the Lord, and prays often, the minister will find it possible to say much in little. Unless some part of his prayer is remembered, it may do little good. In pastoral calling, as in the sanctuary, a flow of words, devoid of facts, may be worth no more than it costs. On the other hand, the minister should not be " flowery." Indirectly he should show the friends how to conduct family devotions. Sometimes they hesitate to do so because they cannot speak in the pastor's unearthly language. If so, thank God! Why not talk things over with the Heavenly Father?

Many a minister has begun writing out a brief prayer every morning. By doing so he is able to control wandering thoughts. He can also learn to use words that prove fitting in prayer. Constantly " educated ministers " need to remember that prayer and praise call for the expression of feeling, not merely thought. When the heart is moved aright, the words flow in a pleasing rhythm. In short, if a man wishes to excel as a pastor, he must learn to pray with ordinary people.

Each morning during his devotions, the minister can put on paper the substance of a prayer to be offered in certain homes the same afternoon. The words need not be committed to memory. The act of writing them out, after he has decided what to say, will help to fix in mind what he will need in any home. From one house to another the form will vary according to the needs. All the while the leader should remember that Christian prayer means sacrifice. Then he may determine with David:

" Neither will I offer . . . unto the Lord my God of that which doth cost me nothing " (II Sam. 24:24).

Here follows a prayer written out in the study but never used elsewhere: " O Lord, we thank Thee for this home. We bless Thee for the father, the mother, and the children, whom we remember before Thee. [Name them one by one, slowly.] We pray especially for Thomas, far away across the sea. Keep him in Thy tender care. Make him strong and true. Enable him to live and serve as a soldier of the Cross. Use him and our other sons in causing righteousness to prevail and peace to return throughout the world that our Saviour died to redeem. *Model*

" We ask Thee also to bless our church. Look in favor on this Thy servant as she gives her time and love in the Sunday School. Strengthen her husband in all his labors for Christ and the Church. Grant Thy Spirit to the younger children as they grow more like the Lord Jesus. Hear us now as we pray together." (Repeat slowly the Lord's Prayer.) *Model*

This period of devotion may lead up to the Benediction of Light (Num. 6:24–26). In case of special need it may seem better to close with the Benediction of Peace (Heb. 13:20, 21), or a majestic doxology (Jude 24, 25). In family prayers, as in the sanctuary, why use only one benediction? Should not the words at the end of the period accord with what has gone before? If spoken aright, almost any Biblical benediction or doxology will form the climax of the pastoral call.

The posture depends on the customs of the denomination and the background of the family. Certain folk with a Lutheran tradition may prefer to stand for the prayer. This posture lends itself admirably to a few words Godward just before one leaves. They will lead up to the Apostles' Creed, followed by the Benediction of Light. Sometimes it seems fitting to bow down while still seated. Among friends with Scottish ancestry the custom in family worship has been to kneel. The difficulty here is that one may pray too long. On the other hand, kneeling sets an example of what the friends should do night and morning before they leave the table.

Never make them feel embarrassed if they do not kneel in prayer

Such pastoral devotions may lead up to a collect. If so, it should be committed to memory, and spoken word for word. If the visit comes late in the afternoon, the going down of the sun may suggest the content of the prayer. In a household that seems to lie beneath deepening shadows, one may utter the beautiful words that appear below. Ordinarily one should dwell more on the sunny side of Christian faith. But at times there is need of this prayer composed by John Henry Newman:

" O Lord, support us all the day long of this our troublous life, until the shadows lengthen, and the evening comes, and the busy world is hushed, and the fever of life is over, and our work is done. Then of Thy mercy grant us a safe lodging, and a holy rest, and peace at the last; through Jesus Christ our Lord. Amen."

Model

Suggested Readings

Baillie, John, *A Diary of Private Prayer*. Charles Scribner's Sons, 1936.
Stewart, George, *A Face to the Sky*. Association Press, 1940.
Suter, John W., Jr., *The Book of English Collects*. Harper & Brothers, 1941.

a great danger of repitition in prayer - moreso than preaching - offering variety - an act of worship.

Simplicity

Contents -
1. Blessing on home every member named (usually)
2. relation of family to church.
3. close with a Benediction - (Suggestive)

IX

The Reading from the Bible

Is it wise to read from the Book just before one offers prayer? Here again, who can lay down rules? Often one may simply quote a verse or two, such as Matt. 11:28–30. Then one can repeat some of the same words the second time, to fix them firmly in the friends' minds. One may also write them on the back of a calling card, and leave them at parting. Whatever the procedure, or the passage, the words from the Bible should come before the prayer. This and the benediction should conclude the pastoral call. Then one ought to leave quietly, if such a course proves feasible.

The reading ought to be informal, though not slovenly, or automatic. A man does not pull out the Bible as though it were a pistol. Rather should the approach be deliberate and cheerful: "In the light of what you have been saying, let me read a few words from the Book." If there is in the room near at hand a copy of the Bible, or else the New Testament and The Psalms, why not read from that? Where the pages have already been marked, one can put a light pencil check opposite the portion used, and then leave the book open at the place. If the volume has not been marked, it is better to write out on a card the location of the passage, and then leave the card in the Bible.

Ordinarily the minister uses his own copy of the New Testament and The Psalms. They should be bound together. The type ought to be large enough to permit reading in a room dimly lighted. The pages are easier to turn and mark if not composed of India paper. This little book the minister carries in his breast pocket, where he might otherwise have a fluted handkerchief. He ought to be so familiar with the contents, and with the location of the golden passages, that he can turn to any part quickly. In the course of a year's calling he should employ chosen portions of almost every book in the New Testament. Especially will he find in The Psalms his " vade mecum."

  1. *The Choice of the Passage.*   The value of the reading depends much on how well it fits the occasion and meets the need. Before one starts forth on afternoon rounds one should have in mind a portion of Scripture to which one will turn unless conditions in a certain home call for something else. The selection may be influenced by the season of the year. In the springtime, if the people love to work in the garden, one may read the parable about the four kinds of soil (Matt. 13:1–9, 18–23).[1] If so, one passes by verses that there is not time to explain. What remains will prove long enough, if not too long, for use in a pastoral call.

  In the autumn one may choose the First Psalm, with its word pictures of the fruitful tree and the worthless chaff. Before the reading one can explain that this little song provides the keynote for the book of The Psalms. This opening portion tells about the blessedness of being good. During the period before Thanksgiving one may read the Eighty-fifth Psalm, or the Sixty-fifth. Still better would be the One Hundred and Twenty-first, the Traveler's Psalm; or the Ninety-first. Best of all, for some of us, would be the One Hundred and Third. Especially do the first thirteen verses sing about the loving-kindness of our God.

  In coming chapters we shall consider ways of using the Bible in solving special problems. Beneath practically all of them in our day lies the fact of war, with its aftermath. That may call for the reading of the Forty-sixth Psalm. In fact, " the treasury of David " abounds in golden passages, many of them short, which enable the pastor to meet almost every human need with words of beauty revealing the heart of God. All the while a man's own soul ought to be fed and refreshed by these words full of grace and truth. How could a minister do his work from day to day if he did not know and love the New Testament and The Psalms?

Sometimes the choice of the reading is suggested by the current stage of the Christian year. Early in December God's people should be thinking about the Advent of our Lord. What Scripture could be more appropriate than one of the beautiful songs about His birth? Especially in days of war and rebuilding there may be a crying need for the truths contained in the Benedictus (Luke 1:68–79). The more one learns about human griefs, and about the Book of Books, the more one feels that the Scriptures are profitable for all things. They have the promise of the life that now is, and of that which is to come.

In our times many a local minister is learning to enjoy preaching from the Bible. Every few months he may single out a certain book and ask his lay friends to read it in their homes. Then he promises to use it as the basis of his morning sermons during the coming weeks. When he calls at this season, naturally he will prefer to read from the book that his friends are enjoying. Of course the chosen part may not be from the New Testament or The Psalms. If so, perhaps he can borrow from them a copy of the Scriptures. In any case, the pastor can serve as the household advocate of reading the Bible as it was written, book by book. For example, the part in hand may be one of the four Gospels. Where is the human need that the Bible-loving minister cannot meet by using a portion of St. Mark, or St. Luke?

Sometimes special conditions in the home call for a certain kind of passage. Here is a concrete case. Near Columbus, Ohio, a young man and his wife were driving in their coupé along the west bank of the Scioto River. All at once the kingbolt dropped out of the steering gear. Soon the automobile plunged into the stream, where the water was twenty feet deep. Neither of them could swim. Nevertheless, they escaped, almost as by a miracle. Within an hour after they had arrived at home, bruised and shocked, the pastor stood at their door.

When the young wife saw him, she exclaimed: " Come in and offer thanks for our deliverance from death! " What passage of Scripture he employed he does not recall. He might

have spoken from memory a few verses from the One Hundred
and Seventh Psalm. There the stress falls on the two refrains,
each of which sounds out four times: "They cried unto the
Lord in their trouble, and he saved them out of their dis-
tresses"; "Oh that men would praise the Lord for his goodness, and for his wonderful works to the children of men!"

2. *The Reading of the Word.* Under God, the value of
the reading may depend a good deal on how it is done. How
can one interpret a passage unless one knows what it means?
The lack of prior study may account for the way one often
mumbles and stumbles and blunders over imaginary bumps. In
a private home, as in the sanctuary, the reading of the written
Word should be deliberate. The stress ought to fall on the verb
and the noun, not the preposition and the pronoun. In the
reading from Holy Scripture a misplaced emphasis or a lack
of rhythm may be as distressing as the syncopation of a sonata
from Beethoven. Surely "God made not anything at all so
beautiful as words."

As a rule the passage ought to be short. If a son of the household is on active duty over in the Mediterranean, one can use
the central part of the twenty-seventh chapter in the book
of The Acts. One can tell the friends that this passage contains
the world's most wondrous description of a storm at sea. Then
one can read verses 20–25, inclusive. The part stressed most
should be the words of the apostle: "Be of good cheer: for I
believe God." If the reader has done his work well, this chapter ought to become one of the household favorites.

It is better to use one passage than several. Our lay friends
are already confused and perplexed because of our hop-skip-
and-jump way of running about in the Holy Scriptures. Why
not show them, time after time, the way to approach the Bible as a collection of books? Within any one part, why not
single out a certain unit, and then make it glow? [1] Instead of
continually exhorting people to read the Bible, and scolding
them for not doing so, why not show them how? After every
call in a home why not leave in their hearts another illuminated
portion of Holy Writ?

Someone may ask, " Why read, and not quote? " Of course the minister should speak out of his heart a good deal of Scripture as he goes among the people. Not to do so would seem as strange as if a golfer who plays under par never once alluded to his favorite sport, or as if a newly made grandfather did not once refer to the last of his namesakes. The difficulty is that by quoting Scripture a man may call attention to himself and his working knowledge of the Book. Unless he has become blind through poring over its pages, he does well to read where he might quote. Is he not striving to show his friends how to use the Bible in the home? A Bible-reading pastor should lead to a Bible-loving people.

After a few words from the Book, one may echo them in prayer. As a rule the man who excels in prayer does not keep quoting Scripture. Still his petitions ought to contain a saturated solution of Biblical truths in beautiful forms. If he has just read about a deliverance from peril on the sea, he should not begin to pray about a dry and thirsty land. His prayers may be extempore in form, but they ought to proceed from a heart in tune with the melody that has sounded forth from God's Holy Book. " Blessed is he that readeth, and they that hear the words of this prophecy, and keep the things which are written therein " (Rev. 1:3).

3. *The Record of the Readings.* When the minister enters a home he should have clearly in mind what he has read there previously, especially in his latest call. On the back of the card showing the names of the persons in the household, he should have jotted down the date of each successive call, and the location of the passage read. Before he goes to the home a glance at the card will show what he should not use, at least not without knowing he has done so before. If he has kept no such record, he may have chosen the Twenty-third Psalm half a dozen times in succession. Fortunately, that song about the Good Shepherd never grows old. But should not the parish interpreter be able to bring forth something different each time?

A case will show the need of a simple record. Mother Scott had become blind so late in life that she could not master the

Braille. She received excellent care from the other members of the household, except that they often left her alone in her darkness. One afternoon she was glad to hear the voice of her pastor. She had welcomed his coming only a few times, as he was new in the parish. During a happy conversation about the things of God, he learned much that he has prized through the years. Then he said to her, gently: " What shall I read? Perhaps I used this psalm the last time I was here."

" No, dominie," said the dear old Scottish woman, " you chose the Ninety-first Psalm. The time before that you read the Nineteenth. At your second call you did not read or pray. The first time you read part of the closing chapter in Philippians." After those simple words, not intended as a rebuke, the young man struggled through the Scripture and the prayer. Before he stole away he kissed the aged saint on the forehead. On the way home he made this resolve: " By the grace of God I shall never again leave such a thirsty soul without having read from the Book and offered a prayer." Then he made another vow: " I shall never use the same passage twice without having some reason for doing so." Should a pastor ever act like a parrot?

4. The Minister's Knowledge of the Book. Everywhere one hears a just complaint: " The seminary did not teach us how to use the Bible in meeting the needs of men." Except for the failure in pastoral theology, this other lack may have been the seminary's most serious sin of omission. Ofttimes the two go together. The school that teaches the Bible impractically does not train men to be pastors. Fortunately, both defects are being remedied. As for the men now on the field, any of them who employs the Bible for a few years in preparing to preach and in doing pastoral work will gain a working knowledge of the Holy Scriptures.

Such a mastery of the Book helps to make a man a worthy pastor. Being a good shepherd, in turn, causes him to glean more and more from the Book. As John Ruskin used to insist, no part of Holy Writ can rightly be understood apart from a deed. Out in the homes of the parish the student of the Word

90% – children from Church.
10% – converted from outsid

can find a demonstration garden. There he can show the meaning of one passage after another, as well as the value in the lives of men and women today.

Every week or so some one or another of our graduates comes in to report about his progress out in the harvest field. No one brings the teacher more joy than the pastor who has learned how to use the Book in helping people to find God as a very present help in time of trouble. Such a minister shows the meaning of what the aged apostle once wrote to young Timothy, who had taken charge of a local church. The preceding verses relate to his knowing the written Word: " The man of God will be adequate, and equipped for any good work " (II Tim. 3:17, Goodspeed's Translation).

Suggested Readings

Curry, S. S., *Vocal and Literary Interpretation of the Bible*. George H. Doran Company, 1903.

Green, Peter, *The Devotional Use of the Bible*. S. P. C. K., London, 1939.

Love, Julian P., *How to Read the Bible*. The Macmillan Company, 1940.

Richardson, Alan, *A Preface to Bible Study*. The Westminster Press, 1944.

X

The Art of Winning Children

WHO can estimate the importance of children in the church? The discussion here concerns them with reference to the pastor. For his sake, as well as theirs, he should often " read, mark, learn, and inwardly digest " the classic work by Horace Bushnell, *Christian Nurture*.[1] Every minister should ponder its famous thesis: " The child is to grow up a Christian, and never know himself as being otherwise." A present-day writer would have stated the fact in the plural. Bushnell, however, illustrated what he called " the individualizing power." That is a prime essential in pastoral work.

Certain other statements from that book call for emphasis: " Let every Christian father and mother know, when their child is three years old, that they have done more than half they will ever do for his character." " More is done . . . before the age of language than after." " Home and religion are kindred words: home, because it is the seat of religion; religion, because it is the sacred element of home." " Family religion makes the families so many little churches." " The house, having in it a domestic spirit of grace, should become the church of childhood." " A house without a roof would scarcely be a more indifferent home than a family without religion."

Some of these sayings might lead the young minister astray. According to Bushnell himself, they were not intended to discourage adult evangelism. In large measure what the sage of Hartford wrote about boys and girls a hundred years ago still holds true. If so, who ought to impress these facts on the father and mother? The pastor! That seems to be one of his chief privileges. Both in the pulpit and through house-to-house visitation he should promote family religion.

Once again give heed to Bushnell. Speaking about marriage,

he devotes a chapter to " The Out-Populating Power of the Christian Stock." What does this mean? Simply that if parents and pastor working together bring to a saving experience of Jesus Christ all the boys and girls within the families of every local church, the Kingdom of God will soon come on earth. In view of such lofty ideals, no minister should delegate to others his portion in the nurture of boys and girls, one by one. What, then, should he do as the shepherd of these lambs in the flock?

1. The pastoral nurture of a child should *begin before he is born.* In fact, it should start long before his parents are wed. If they have been nurtured aright, they should become worthy parents. As such they need the tender concern of the minister and his wife during the months of waiting for the supreme event in all their household history, the coming of the first-born child. It was so in the case of Edward and Margaret, for whom the pastor felt unusual concern. With joy he had officiated at their marriage. About a year later, one evening they called at the manse and visited on the front porch. There in the darkness the young wife told the mistress of the manse a precious secret.

Because of that " pastoral call," in reverse, the two homes meant still more to each other. When at last the baby was born, each of the exultant grandmothers telephoned the pastor. He expressed his joy, and asked the mother's mother to let him know when he could call at the hospital to see the baby. Then the minister got in touch with the father to extend felicitations. All the parties concerned, including the newly made grandparents, should enter into the picture at this happy stage in the work of the minister. At such a time he may read with interest the Christmas sermon by Dr. Harry Emerson Fosdick, " The Decisive Babies of the World." [2]

Five days after the birth of the child, the maternal grandmother notified the pastor that he could call at the hospital. This he did the same afternoon, traveling out eight miles to be there when the visiting hours started at two o'clock. Then he made other visits on the way home, for he did not tarry long in that upper room. After a few minutes of quiet talk with the mother, he asked if he could see the baby. (All this might not be possible at other places of healing. In some parts of Canada, except during an emergency, no one but the physician and the nurse is supposed to visit the maternity ward.)

The young nurse brought wee Martha and laid her down in the mother's arms. The minister knelt for a verse of Scripture and a few words of prayer. He thanked God for watching over the mother and babe during the months that had gone. He likewise remembered the father and the others in the family circles. After the benediction the pastor arose, kissed the baby on the top of her head, and stole out of the room with never a word. He wished to leave mother and child alone with the Lord.

A few days later the minister called again at the hospital. There he was greeted by the maternal grandmother. With glee she related an experience with the Roman Catholic nurse: " Last Tuesday as soon as you were out of sight she came rushing in and said to my daughter, ' Is little Martha going to die? ' ' No,' replied the mother, ' I think not. Why do you ask? ' ' Because they never send for the *father* unless the baby is about to die! ' ' Oh, is that all? You know we are Protestants. Our minister has taught us that if God takes a baby home to heaven He will keep her there in safety and peace. But if He leaves her here He wishes us to train her for Him and the Church.' "

Six months afterward, on Easter morning, Edward and Margaret brought little Martha to the House of the Lord for baptism. There they dedicated her publicly to the service of the One from whom she had come to bless their home. If the pastor had continued in the field he would have followed the procedure outlined below. Doubtless his successor pursued such a course of Christian nurture. At all events as a college graduate young Martha today shows the influence of loving care that began before she was conceived in the womb. Such experiences tend to justify the title of the book by Dr. Raymond Calkins, *The Romance of the Ministry*. Would that such events were not uncommon!

2. The pastor's loving care should *lead the growing child to love the home church*. Of course one takes for granted the hearty co-operation of both the parents, as well as the teachers in the Bible School. Here we can think only about the pastor. Time would fail us to consider methods of promoting church attendance on the part of boys and girls. If we succeeded in that endeavor, we might solve the most critical problem of the typical congregation, that of irregular attendance by its members. How can we hope to win the world for Christ when the majority of our own people seldom darken the doors of the sanctuary? Probably they did not form the habit as little children.

Pastoral nurture of boys and girls becomes most active during the months leading up to the confirmation of baptismal vows. Opinions differ concerning the age when these young friends should be welcomed to the Lord's Supper. Doubtless some ought to apply for full church membership earlier than others. Certain pastors think of ten years as the norm. Others, especially among the Dutch, prefer sixteen, or eighteen. The present writer agrees with his youngest son, who asked permission to join the pastor's class when twelve years of age. The lad wished to confirm the baptismal vows when he had reached the age of our Lord at the Temple. " Know ye not that I must be in my Father's house? "

Every wide-awake minister thinks in terms of a pastor's class. He may prefer this title, rather than " communicants' class." That suggests the necessity of uniting with the Church. The shorter name stresses the minister's desire to shepherd the lambs of the flock. Ideally, in a parish of any size, he would prefer to have two classes, or even more. One way to do that is for the pastor to teach the boys and then let his wife deal with the girls. If the group is large, there may be another class for young folk of teen age. Still a fourth group might be for adults. This is partly what one means by " a teaching ministry." Here we can think only about the class, or classes, for young boys and girls.

Ideally, the pastor's class should extend over several years.

Actually, the period may include only eight weeks. If so, the best time to start may be after New Year's, so as to culminate with the public reception of these new members on Palm Sunday. What a time for the recruits to put on the uniform of King Jesus! Was it not on the first Palm Sunday that boys and girls in old Jerusalem sang glad hosannas to the King of Kings? Meanwhile the pastor should guide them, one by one, in the desire to come out boldly on the side of the Redeemer.

How can the minister attract young friends to the first meeting of the group? By careful planning, as well as work, both in their homes and at the Church School. There he should enlist the help of the officers and the teachers in the departments concerned. Through their aid he can secure a list showing the names and addresses of all the boys and girls whom he ought to invite. To each of them he should send a personal letter, which he ought to sign with a pen, not with a rubber stamp. The letter may be typed, but it should not be mimeographed. It should be on the regular stationery of the church and go out under first-class postage. In dealing with sensitive boys and girls, do not be niggardly.

The typical lad or lass twelve years of age may not receive a " sure-enough " letter once in three months. Such a message from the pastor should constitute an event. Even in a local church that does not practice infant baptism a letter like the one below would prove helpful. So would a class for the boys and girls whom the deacons consider mature enough to accept Christ as Saviour and then be buried with Him in baptism. However we may differ about the Biblical route to the goal, we all wish our growing sons and daughters consciously and gladly to become followers of Christ as Saviour and Lord. Into the preparation of this letter should go almost as much time and prayer as into many a message for adults. The heading should be as to a grown-up friend. After the address, " My dear John," or " My dear Mary," one can say:

" You are invited to join the Pastor's Class next Friday at 3:45 P.M. Please come to the study a little before that time, on your way home from school. The class will start promptly at 3:45, and will close at 4:30. We shall meet at 3:45 every Friday for eight weeks.

" The purpose of the class is to find out what it means for a boy like you to be a Christian. As a guide we shall use a little book that you can secure at the class for fifteen cents. This book will help you learn about Jesus.

" Another purpose is to aid me in getting to know you better as one of my friends. At the same hour on Friday, Mrs. Blackwood will meet with the girls. At the end of the last meeting we hope to entertain both classes in our home.

" Please talk about this matter tonight with your father and mother. Next Sunday take it up with your Bible School teacher. In former years I have enjoyed being with the boys in the group. Come next Friday and make this class the best ever.

" Your pastor and friend,"

_____.

With the group in class the minister tried to be informal. Still he preserved order. When some of the boys became restless he would have the whole class arise and repeat something in concert. The materials that follow show the gist of what he taught the boys who were thinking about confessing Christ and thus becoming communicant members of His Church. At the public welcome of these new recruits on Palm Sunday he asked the boys and girls some of the questions below. Since they did not know which ones were coming, they learned the whole list by heart. Thus the entire congregation heard anew what it means to be a Christian soldier.

1. Who is Jesus Christ? The *Son of God and the Saviour of the world.*
2. What does He do for us Christians and for our world? He *reveals the Father — redeems from sin — rules as Lord.*
3. What has He done for us in Middletown? He has given us — *Christian homes — churches — schools — ideals — service.*
4. What is it to become a Christian? To accept Him as *my Teacher — my Saviour — my Master.*

 5. Memorize John 3:16 — Matt. 5:16 — Matt. 6:33 (King James Version).
 6. How can I confess Jesus Christ? *In my daily life — in the hour of temptation — by joining His Church.*
 7. How can I unite with His Church? *By confessing Him, and by promising in His strength to lead a Christian life.*
 8. Why should I join His Church? To honor Him by — *advancing His Kingdom — building up His Church — helping others — making the most of myself, for His sake.*
 9. Who should belong to His Church? *Every Christian* — everyone who *believes in Him* and wishes to *do His will.*
10. When should I become a Christian and unite with His Church? Now, *when I am young,* so that I may *serve Him all my life.*
11. What is the Church? The *home of God's children* in the world.
12. What are the duties of Church members? To honor Him by — *leading a Christian life — loyalty to His Church — Christian service every day.*
13. Name the two sacraments. *Baptism* and the *Lord's Supper.*
14. What is baptism? The way the believer *confesses Christ* and *publicly joins His Church.*
15. What is the Lord's Supper? The way we Christians publicly show our *love for Christ and His Cross.*
16. Name five other means of Christian growth. *Bible-reading — prayer — church attendance — Christian friendship — Christian work.*
17. What portion of my income should I set apart for religion and benevolences, especially missions? At least *one tenth.*
18. What should determine my choice of a lifework? I should seek *— to do the will of God — be useful to my fellow men —* and *make the most of my life, for His sake.*
19. How can I be sure to know my duty and be strong to do it? *He will show me* what I should do, and *make me strong* to do it well — if I trust Him day by day.

3. The young minister should also *study the ways of other churches.* For example, take the Lutherans. Why has their branch of the Church been growing more rapidly in our country than any other Protestant group? Largely because the Lutherans excel in pastoral nurture, especially among boys and girls. According to Martin Luther, the chief mark of the worthy minister is the ability to " teach systematically." [3] For

a practical commentary on the statement turn to the autobiography of Dr. Albert Schweitzer, medical missionary in Africa.[4] As a lad he was prepared for confirmation by an elderly pastor whom young Albert had revered.

The minister's instruction proved to be excellent. It suggested all sorts of problems: " How many questions I should gladly have asked him, but that was not allowed." (The place to answer such questions is in the study, at some other time, when the lad is alone with his friend the pastor.) To Albert's amazement he learned indirectly that the minister thought the lad was " going through confirmation as one of the indifferent ones." " In reality I was during those weeks so moved by the holiness of the time that I felt almost ill."

On Palm Sunday the organist played from Handel's *Messiah* " Lift Up Your Heads, O Ye Gates! " To this majestic music the young recruits marched from the vestry into the main sanctuary. There for the first time they entered the service of Christ as King. Years later the missionary hero wrote about the effect of that class on his work as a young minister:

" As assistant pastor in Strassburg for ten years I gave confirmation instruction to boys. How often, when any of them seemed indifferent, have I had to think of dear old Dr. W. and myself, and remind myself that much more goes on in a child's heart than others are allowed to suspect. I always took pains to make the boys feel that they could come to me about anything that troubled them. Twice a week was given to answering questions they put to me." Is not this the way to win boys now? As for the girls, why not turn them over to " the shepherdess "?

Much the same loving nurture should be given these friends during the difficult adolescent years when they are learning how to " put away childish things." What they most need may be sympathy. That the minister can supply if he remains young at heart. In the life of almost every teen-age youth or maiden there comes a time when " nobody seems to care." What if the minister can make it clear that the Lord Jesus once was this

very age? Was He not " in all points tempted like as we are,
yet without sin "? " What a Friend we have in Jesus, all our
sins and griefs to bear! "

4. Pastoral nurture means to *love the boys and girls.* How
else could one serve as their leader? The man with the shepherd
heart learns to look on everything human or divine as it concerns these young friends. When the writer was leaving the
pastorate to become a full-time professor, he received a tribute
that he loves to recall. The clerk of the presbytery, or " local
conference," said in public: " I have listened to this man leading in prayer on all sorts of occasions. Never once have I failed
to hear him plead for God's blessing on little boys and girls."
In more recent years he has fallen from grace.

How does the pastor show love for these young friends? He
knows them all, one by one, according to their given names. He
believes in them, just as they are. Seldom does he refer to them
as " children." What growing lad of ten or twelve wishes to
be addressed as " a child "? The pastor makes every one of them
feel that God expects much from this growing friend. By experience and observation the minister knows that these tender years seldom prove the happiest in life. Only the dreamer
with eyes fixed on distant vistas would sing with Wordsworth:

> " Heaven lies about us in our infancy!
> Shades of the prison-house begin to close
> Upon the growing Boy."

That should never come to pass in a Christian home and
church Under the loving eyes of parents and pastor these
young friends ought to grow " in wisdom and stature, and in
favour with God and man " — more and more like Jesus. To
the loving eye of the shepherd, any of them seems more precious than gold. When he devotes himself to the nurture of
boys and girls he is laying up treasures in heaven. Meanwhile
his young friends should be making ready to do their part in
building a better world.

Suggested Readings

Jones, Mary Alice, *The Faith of Our Children*. Abingdon-Cokesbury
Press, 1943.
Sherrill, Lewis J., *The Opening Doors of Childhood*. The Macmillan
Company, 1939.
Sherrill, Lewis J., *The Rise of Christian Education*. The Macmillan
Company, 1944.

Mother's Day — a good
day to dedicate children

— no set form —
make it different + effective
— Particularly — charge
the Parent
Parents are to be pleased — unless
some principle is involved.

time —
  — before service
or — more effective yet —
  as Mother's Day — read
about influence of the home
+ close with the dedication —
so they feel a great responsibility
for the child's nurture + training.
  group — brief + variety
Certificate — New Testament.

XI

The Ways of Attracting Men

WE now come to the most perplexing problem thus far. Every pastor knows the need of attracting men, one by one, and in groups. For his own sake he ought to mingle with them freely, as well as with women and children. For the good of the men also he should seek them out as their pastor and guide. Erelong he should become " a friend that sticketh closer than a brother." Here and there a man of God seems to approach this lofty ideal. One of them appears to be Canon Peter Green, of the downtown cathedral in Manchester, England.

In this man's program for parish work there must be a large place for the men. He insists that it is far from enough to attract women.[1] In fact, he almost makes light of a congregation that does not include more than a few stalwart men. His ideals relate to the number and the proportion of men who come to church week after week and enter into the Lord's work with all their might. Except in days when war removes a host from our midst, the numbers of men in the sanctuary ought to equal those of women. It was so with the present writer in his last two charges.

Canon Green shows elsewhere that a parish minister's ability to attract men for Christ varies according to his personality and his pastoral work.[2] Occasionally a pulpit orator draws throngs of men to enjoy his preaching. Doubtless that has its value in religion. But if they come merely to hear the minister they will absent themselves when he no longer fills the pulpit. Was it not so with T. De Witt Talmage? Whenever he preached, the house was crowded. Many of his admiring auditors were men. As soon as he left Brooklyn, or Washington, D. C., the pews were deserted. Would it not be better to build up a church composed largely of men who love the Lord? That calls for pastoral work.

Such an undertaking bristles with difficulties. The traditions of pastoral care have to do largely with women and children. Especially in days of industrial " triple shifts " it may seem impossible to find busy men at home and free to think about their souls. Worse still, many of them do not wish to be found by the parson. If they do not dread his presence, more or less, they may look on him as harmless, or even as a joke. Whatever the reason, the Protestant ministry has not learned how to reach large numbers of men for Christ and His Kingdom. In the discussion here we shall think of the problem only as it relates to pastoral work.

1. At the very least every parish minister should *attract men indirectly.* First of all, he should gain and hold their respect for himself as a man. By this one means a strong Christian gentleman, not merely a " ladies' man." For a series of word pictures showing the " oily " type of clergyman, whom red-blooded men do not admire, read *Barchester Towers,* by Anthony Trollope. In that realistic novel " Mr. Swope " shows how not to be a pastor:

" With the men he is generally at variance; but with the ladies he is, as he conceives, all-powerful. He can reprove faults with so much flattery that the female heart can not withstand him. He has, however, a pawing, greasy way with him, which does not endear him to those who do not value him for their souls' sake."

In fact, it would be hard to find in fiction a stalwart Protestant clergyman. Where can one discover the non-Catholic counterpart of the bishop in *Les Misérables,* by Victor Hugo, or of Father Chisholm in *The Keys of the Kingdom,* by A. J. Cronin? For Protestant ministerial heroes we must turn to biography. There we find George Herbert and Richard Baxter, Jean F. Oberlin and Thomas Chalmers, Phillips Brooks and Theodore L. Cuyler. No one of those pastors seems to have had difficulty in attracting men as well as women. Wherein such drawing power resides who can tell? The fact remains that laymen here at home like to have as their pastor and friend a minister who would have excelled as a chaplain among the Marines.

The pastor can reach men indirectly by taking good care of their loved ones. It is so with the family physician. How often does he catch a glimpse of many a businessman? Nevertheless, the merchant gives thanks to God for the skillful friend who safeguards the health of the wife and the children. By proxy the minister too can gain a large place in the heart of a loving father. In that case of Edward and Margaret the pastor's attentions were devoted chiefly to the womenfolk and the newborn child. Notwithstanding, the father knew all that was going on. To this day he shares with wife and daughter in esteem for the minister whom he seldom saw except at church on the Lord's Day.

Once again, think of a commercial traveler. From Sunday night until after dark on Friday he must live away from home. During the week the salesman learns that the pastor has cared tenderly for the aged mother in the family circle. In various ways he has shown solicitude for the spiritual welfare of the children. In his prayers when he called, the clergyman invoked the blessing of God on the husband and father as he flitted hither and yon. If you loved that home and everyone there, would you not thank God for this man with the shepherd heart? On the other hand, if he neglected those dear ones, would you not wonder why?

Thomas Carlyle tells about such a masculine servant of God. The burly Scotsman has been describing a man whom he reveres. Then the essayist goes on to declare: " A second man I honor, and still more highly: him who is seen toiling for the spiritually indispensable; not daily bread, but the bread of life. . . . Highest of all, when his outward and inward endeavor are one; when we can name him Artist; not earthly Craftsman only, but inspired Thinker, who with heaven-made implement conquers heaven for us." What an ideal for the pastor today!

2. The minister can also *visit the men at special hours*. Even in days of staggered schedules, many a busy layman can

be found at home during certain hours of the day or week. The wide-awake pastor knows about the working habits of those whom he wishes to reach. He may likewise be aware that some of the laymen dodge the parson. They might like him better if they knew him well. They would understand him aright if they attended church every Sunday. Meanwhile the pastor may wonder how he can break into the circle that shuts him out of such a man's heart.

<u>One way is to call at night</u>. If that is the program, there should be few visits during the afternoon. Two or three hours a day spent among the homes of the people should afford a sufficient tax on any man's nervous energies. Then too he ought to set apart certain times for reading. On any evening except Saturday or Sunday, if there is no meeting to attend, he can visit homes where the men are not at work on early night shifts. He soon finds that he cannot make so many calls in one evening as in an afternoon. <u>On the other hand, he discovers that hearts are more likely to open up after sunset</u>. That may have been one reason why Nicodemus came to see the Master at night. What family will soon forget the kindness of the busy pastor in calling one evening, and the uplift of his closing prayer? Why not plan to do such work whenever possible?

In the Far West the former pastor of a huge congregation recently took the oversight of a flock with three hundred members. In less than a year the church had on the rolls eight hundred persons, with more in sight. <u>The minister is said to have relied largely on reaching the men during Sunday afternoon and evening</u>. Such a program would not be feasible where the pastor conducts a second service, especially after dark. The new field on the coast doubtless lay ready for the harvest. The fact remains that the pastor who is determined to reach men on behalf of Christ and the Church can find a way to their hearts.

<u>In some cases it is possible to call at the office or the store</u>. If the friend in view is an <u>employee</u>, one should speak to him only in passing. Even if the man is completely master of his time,

one ought to know when he is most likely to be free. Sometimes it is possible to make an appointment by telephone, but that might cause others to wonder why the pastor did not phone to them. Whatever the procedure, the layman should feel certain that the minister cares for him as a human being. That is partly why George W. Truett in Dallas gained a mighty hold on the hearts of men as well as women. There many a strong layman feels: Dr. Truett cared for me " personally." What a tribute to the pastor of perhaps the largest Protestant congregation in America!

Time does not permit a discussion of men's brotherhoods and clubs. Often they prove disappointing. The reason may be that the aim is purely social. Among women such groups flourish year after year because the objective continues to be spiritual. The sisters enjoy being together; they keep on coming, however, because collectively they are seeking first the Kingdom of God. Here and there, especially in the South and the West, one finds a spiritual congregation where the men are banded together for service like that of Gideon's three hundred warriors. Among " The Men of the Church " nothing else proves so attractive as applied religion.

Almost every city pastor has tried to reach men by joining outside clubs. As a rule the experience leads to little except the expenditure of time and money. Here is the report of a beloved Episcopal rector in the South, who later became a bishop: " When I first came to this capital city I joined the Chamber of Commerce and every other civic or social club that opened its doors to me. I enjoyed the meetings and the jolly good times. After a while I awoke to the fact that I was getting nowhere with the work in my parish. I concluded that if I did not engage in those other activities, someone else would take my place. But if I neglected my people, no one on earth could do my work there." He quit spreading himself out so thinly that he could make little impression on his people. Is it any wonder that he became a bishop?

After a few years in the ministry such a man feels prompted

to set apart a pastor's hour. To that subject we shall return a little later. In opening the door for quiet conferences with his
friends, one at a time, he bids welcome to the stalwart as well
as the sickly. All the while he shows much concern whenever
one of his male friends becomes ill. " He whom thou lovest is
sick." Perhaps this layman has never before been confined to
his bed. He may have boasted that he never has lost a day from
work because of illness. Suppose that the critical stage of his
malady has passed. Partly because of powerful drugs, he may
feel weak as water. What an opportunity for the pastor! Perhaps he can call every day, late in the afternoon.

Once the writer went to see a young physician. The minister
had often been in the home. More than once he and his wife had
been entertained there at dinner. Still he had never thought
of that busy specialist as being much concerned about religion. There on the bed the pastor found his friend committing
to memory eight golden chapters from the Bible. He was following a list handed out five years before by the gifted teacher
of the Men's Bible Class. Because of that experience, the writer
began to use this means of enlisting laymen for the reading of
the Book. Is it any wonder that he still feels grateful for that
quiet upper room where he discovered the soul of a beloved
physician?

In another parish a prominent layman was not well known
to the minister. One day the pastor learned that this banker
had contracted diphtheria. Although the pastor himself was
not immune, he went at once to the home, which was under
quarantine. There he called late each afternoon. By observing
the sort of precautions the family physician prescribed, the
visitor carried away none of the dreaded bacilli. After the patient became convalescent the two men could sit out in the
garden. Since other callers were not admitted, the pastor could
find his way into a heart that proved richly rewarding.

The same line of thought applies more strongly after a tragic
death in the family circle. Think of a strong man who has begun to live for his son and future successor. Then the blow

falls. Soon the body of the son and heir, the pride and joy of his father's heart, lies out in the churchyard. Is the minister to concern himself only with the womenfolk? Does he not know that the " stern " father too carries a broken heart? Only the exceptional pastor knows how to comfort a reticent elderly man in sorrow. The least the parish minister can do is to seek out this friend and show him how much the home shepherd cares for him personally. If possible, lead him to open up his heart and talk about his " boy." Thus you can gently bring the willing heart close to the Heavenly Father.

The grief may be all the more intense because of a beloved daughter. The recent biography of Henry Clay, by Barbara Mayo,[3] tells about his feeling of desolation when he learned that his married daughter Anne had died in Lexington, Kentucky. At Washington, D. C., in 1835, that mighty man received the word just before Christmas. Immediately he fell down in a faint. When at length he was revived he exclaimed with a heavy sigh: " Every tie in life is broken. Henceforth there is nothing before me in this world but duties." At the time he had almost reached the pinnacle of earthly achievement. He had failed to become President, solely because of sheer honesty. But in a world without the presence of his beloved Anne, what did he care for honors and renown? At the age of fifty-eight he had " lost " all the hopes of his declining years.

The biographer says nothing about Henry Clay's religion or his pastor. What an opportunity that Christian gentleman must have had to comfort the aging statesman! When the Lexington divine called at " Ashland," he could scarcely have seen Mrs. Clay. After the death of Anne, the mother shut herself away from her closest friends. But the minister could have found in the desolate father a heart waiting for a sure word from the land where his beloved made her home. The question is, How well does the local pastor measure up to his opportunity when a strong man of the world gives way to grief and despair?

Another question relates to the pastoral oversight of the young men who come home from service in the armed forces. Here again, the pastor's manhood, or lack of it, will amount to more than any set procedure. As for ways and means of enlisting the young men who ought to become leaders in the local church of tomorrow, that would call for a treatise of its own. The pastor who has excelled as a chaplain, or who would have rendered noble service if he had been so called of God, should meet with no insuperable obstacle in dealing with valiant youths who have laid aside the uniform of their country and have begun to walk again in the quiet paths of peace. Treat them like men! [4]

If any minister longs to excel in attracting men of all ages and kinds, let him study the words of Paul to the elders from Ephesus (Acts 20:17–38). For the nonce we may think of them all as laymen. Why did those strong men revere the apostle? Largely because of his pastoral work in Ephesus. Both publicly and from house to house he had served as the community representative of God. He had won men as well as women. He had shown the men that he loved them, and he found that they almost worshiped him. In like manner today, the minister finds no difficulty in reaching the hearts of strong men whom he has led to the foot of the Cross, and whom he has comforted in the time of grief. Why not become the pastor of men?

Suggested Readings

Calkins, Raymond, *How Jesus Dealt with Men.* Abingdon-Cokesbury Press, 1942.

Chirgwin, M. A., *Into Action.* Livingstone Press, London, 1943. (Post-War Religion.)

The Church and Returning Service Personnel. Federal Council of the Churches of Christ in America, and Christian Commission for Camp and Defense Communities, 297 Fourth Avenue, New York, 1943 (10 cents).

Hutchinson, Paul, *From Victory to Peace.* Willett, Clark & Company, 1943.

XII

The Claims of the Sickroom

THE parish minister gives priority to the sick and the dying. The degree of his attention varies according to the seriousness of the illness. Unfortunately, sickness and death abound at the busiest season of the pastor's year. In February and March, at the height of the harvest season in the Church, the obituary columns of the daily newspapers are fuller than at any other time. Hence the minister should have a plan for this vital part of his work.

Nothing that the clergyman does provides a more searching test of his pastoral skill and intellectual acumen than his care of the sick. He must be able to solve one problem after another without seeming at all perplexed. When he enters a sick chamber he cannot be sure what to expect. But the Lord knows, and He is waiting to guide. Sometimes, however, the parson may not be aware that there is any difficulty. For example, only an educated sense of smell can detect certain things that the minister should know about the one who lies ill. Sometimes the odor suggests the presence of syphilis.

The pastor enters the room as the physician of the soul. If he wishes to reap a spiritual harvest, both on earth and in heaven, he engages in what the Lutherans term " Seelsorge." That means the cure, or the care, of the soul. In time of illness the patient and his loved ones often prove responsive. They are likewise sensitive. If the minister fails to come, or if he falls short after he arrives, their hearts may wax cold. Such a feeling throughout the parish will retard the growth of spiritual fruit. How, then, should the pastor prepare to enter the sickroom?

1. *The Christian Attitude Toward Sickness.* First of all, let him make up his mind about the meaning of illness. It need not represent the will of God. Ofttimes the Lord permits what He

"Divine healing is wonderful but good health is better"
Paul Rees

does not cause. Disease means disorder in the body. Usually such inner confusion does not come from God. Why, then, do we speak of " His holy will " in terms of a tombstone, rather than a wedding ring? Let the pastor's emphasis fall on health rather than sickness. Whatever the reason, most patients recover. In short, think of disease as an enemy to be fought and overcome.[1]

A more practical question occurs to the incoming pastor: How can I learn about serious cases of illness? Largely by being a good pastor. Also by enlisting the aid of certain lay men and women. In each district there should be two such helpers.[2] If the " new " minister gains the reputation of liking to call on the sick, and of knowing how, his friends will keep him informed. Sometimes the news comes directly from the family. Often it issues from one of the neighbors. In seventeen years, if memory serves aright, the author never failed to receive such word but once. That time he did not learn about a funeral that had taken place during his midsummer holiday. Doubtless he was at fault, but he never knew how.

At the beginning of a pastorate one may have to educate the people, indirectly. According to Cabot and Dicks, " Perhaps the last incumbent did not care to visit the sick." Worse still, when he did so, most reluctantly, he may have wrought more harm than good. In such a case why not call him an " encumbrance "? But say it softly, to yourself! " Nothing but good concerning the departed! "

How soon ought one to call? In a critical case, immediately. After the first few months in a parish the minister's informants will tell him about the times and the seasons. Some of the laymen know from sad experience that visiting the sick may be overdone. People rush in when their curiosity is aroused. Hospital authorities err more often in admitting visitors than in almost any other respect. Hence a weary woman in a " private room " once told her minister: " I thank you for waiting until Tuesday. I had twenty-two callers Sunday afternoon, and some of them stayed long. It took me all of Monday to re-

Stand for prayer in Hospital
ask how long you might stay; then only stay half as long.

cover the ground I lost on Sunday." " O day of rest and gladness! " Not in many a hospital room!

The eager young pastor may not know how to call at a hospital. One such man of zeal recently went barging into a room where a strange woman was not attired to receive a male visitor. Why not follow a set procedure? At the first call make yourself known to the young woman at the desk. Give her the printed card showing your name and that of the church. Ask if it is convenient for you to see the superintendent a minute or two. From him, or someone else at the office, ascertain the regulations of the hospital. This whole matter should take only a little time. Ever afterward cultivate the friendship of these busy folk.

The friend at the desk will tell the number of the room. She may even show where the doctors leave their hats and overcoats. If not, carry these things on your arm. At the proper floor speak to the nurse in charge. Receive her approval before going into the sickroom. In short, co-operate with those responsible for the bodily welfare of the patient. The same principles apply to the local physicians and surgeons. Cultivate their friendship. Remember that they are busy men, but that they appreciate the helpfulness of a minister who wants to do teamwork in caring for the sick.

The spirit of co-operation often extends further. Here is a case. When the late John McDowell served as pastor of Brown Memorial Church in Baltimore, he learned that in one of the homes a little girl had contracted typhoid fever. There he ministered to her daily until she died. Then he kept on doing everything in his power to comfort the grief-stricken household. Immediately after his first call, without complaining to them or anyone else, he at once visited the Board of Health, where he got the action desired. If he had failed there, he would have gone to the chief of police, or the mayor. The city officials traced the contagion to its source, and then they removed the cause. They also thanked the pastor for dealing with the matter quietly, as a Christian gentleman. He had simply followed the Golden Rule.

The business of calling on the sick usually proves far less formidable than one might suppose. Especially in a case not critical, the sick friend may tarry at home. There the barriers should be down. Even so, a tactful minister remembers that the friends may not be able to secure a nurse. In such a case, they are likely to feel overworked, and their nerves may give way. In view of these facts, the man who calls on the sick must learn how to get along with all sorts of petulant complainers. Here again, he ought to show the inner meaning of the Golden Rule. It guides him in knowing when to call, and how to proceed as the physician of the soul. It likewise teaches him never to apologize for coming in the name of the One who can make this friend " perfectly whole."

2. *The Approach to the Sickroom.* Before entering the sick chamber the minister should learn certain facts. Except when a friend lies at the point of death, there should be time for a little talk with the nurse, or someone else who knows. Such a conversation ought to be held at a distance from the sickroom. Nothing could be more upsetting to a nervous patient than to hear the pastor conversing in stage whispers outside the door. Since the words would not be audible, the one in bed might give way to fears. In fact, many persons when ill seem to dread the approach of the pastor. His sepulchral demeanor makes them think about the funeral director and the Judgment Day.

On the other hand, jollity may be out of place. In dealing with elderly persons who are chronic invalids, humor — though never horseplay — may prove to be an asset. But in serious sickness, especially if acute, when there is much fever with a rapid pulse, the pastor needs to be sympathetic rather than jovial. A case will show one reason. Not long ago in a remote city the author was asked to visit a sick woman whom he had never seen. He found her sitting up in bed, and looking " well."

He was tempted to speak facetiously about something or other. Fortunately, he noticed that the daughter could scarcely restrain her tears. Within two weeks he was called back to that home to conduct the mother's funeral. All the while the daughter knew that internal cancer had almost finished its course. If he had told a funny story or two, would he later have been asked to bring the comfort of God? How can He bless a dislocated sense of humor?

In that case the visitor could not ascertain the facts before he entered the room. The mother had been ill for months, and her bed had been carried downstairs. When the daughter opened the door to greet the strange minister, the mother could hear everything that was said. Hence it would not have been prudent to ask for a private interview. Under such circumstances one acts on a certain principle: These friends take the illness seriously; so shall I. However, there should be no evidence of gloom or alarm. The more radiant the minister appears, the more will he do good. The radiance ought to be that of Christian love, not Sunny Jim jollity or Pollyanna " piety."

What does the minister wish to learn before he enters the sickroom? Ordinarily he leaves such matters to the other person. The nurse, or the friend in charge, will tell him what she thinks he ought to know. This may include the character of the disease, the stage of progress, the length of call deemed best, and perhaps the word that the sick friend has become unconscious. If one has never previously led in prayer at the home, it may be wise to ask if one should do so now. At all events one should listen attentively, and remember what one hears. Then one should resolve to tarry in the room half as long as the person in charge expects. One should also be able to control one's features, so as not to go in as the harbinger of death or the messenger of despair. Look like a Christian!

These assumptions have to do with critical illness. Most maladies yield to treatment. For instance, if a boy suffers from an attack of the mumps, and has no fever, the approach to what he deems a prison cell should be entirely different. In

Olive oil - anointing oil.
→ a little bottle in pocket
alone or with another minister

[handwritten annotation]

[handwritten annotation]

short, size up the situation. Then go on in faith. Under God, the good a minister does in the sickroom depends largely on belief in himself as the servant of the divine Physician. Let this be the spirit in which the pastor approaches the sick friend:

> " The healing of His seamless dress
> Is by our beds of pain;
> We touch Him in life's throng and press,
> And we are whole again."

Occasionally entrance will be denied. If so, do not feel hurt. The physician in charge may have lost confidence in the ability of the local clergy to help in time of crisis. The patient may be asleep. There may be any one of a hundred reasons why nerve-racked folk do not admit a strange minister, or even a pastor of long standing. His way of receiving such news will go far to make his presence welcome the next time he calls. Unless he is asked not to return until notified, he does come back, at least to inquire for the one he wishes to help. Meanwhile the minister prays to the Father, who can bless the friend not visited.

3. *The Call in the Sickroom.* Here again there can be no set rules. A book agent may commit to memory a set of pre-digested statements, a Roman priest may follow his rubrics, but a Protestant pastor should have no fixed " technique." At least there need be none unless the friend seems to be dying.[3] There may be one best way of setting a broken bone, but there can be no hard-and-fast procedure with a sensitive soul. Herein lie the fascination and the difficulty of calling on the sick. Even so, a few suggestions will make clear what often occurs.

If the patient wishes to talk, let her do so. She may indulge in an " organ recital." Very well, her running account should guide the minister in knowing what to say when his time comes. If he has ever suffered from a serious illness he knows the worth of the visitor who keeps quiet, and listens with a responsive spirit. Meanwhile the temptation recurs to break into the stream of talk: " That reminds me of my own experience "; " Your case resembles —." Why interrupt? With a

sick friend, as with a child, let her alone for a while. She is enjoying the invalid's privilege — that of occupying the pulpit.
Remember that the last word will rest with you. It may well
be one of prayer and benediction. If so, the prayer should relate to what you have learned during " the early part of the
service."

Why does the pastor come into the sickroom? Partly to show
the ill friend that God cares. Little by little, after the first rush
of talk, the minister can usually guide the conversation into
channels more or less religious. At least he can try. It is not his
province to help the patient to diagnose the malady. The pastor should never suggest a favorite remedy or a change of
physicians. Neither should he express any opinion about the
progress of the disease. In matters strictly medical, do not
meddle. Meanwhile there must be at least one truth of religion
that the friend needs to know. When that lesson has come
forth, perhaps indirectly, the pastor should make ready to
leave. First, however, there ought to be a " spiritual prescrip-
tion."

Normally, such a call leads up to a brief portion of Scripture, or perhaps a hymn, and a few words of prayer, with the
Lord's Prayer, and the benediction. If by making the suggestion about prayer one would alarm the patient, one waits for
a more convenient season. However, the spiritually-minded
pastor soon gains the reputation, locally, of praying with
friends who are not about to die. Perhaps he knelt with this
one when he first called at the home. If so, the natural way for
the physician of the soul to end a hospital call should be to in-
voke the blessing of God the Father.

The real good may be done after the initial call. An English
writer tells of a young husband and father who lay dying with
cancer. The physician expected him to live two months,
whereas he lasted six. The wife told the pastor that her husband did not wish to see any clergyman. Hence the minister
strove first to foster good will. This he and his women workers
did by showing kindness to the three children and their mother.

Erelong he gained access to the sick chamber. Gradually he led the dying man to acceptance of the Saviour. Then the clergyman administered the Sacrament. Later he received into Church membership the wife and her sister. The small children were enrolled in the Church School. What a parish comforter and guide!

The large majority of sick persons recover. An Episcopal rector in the South once kept accurate account of the " cures " wrought in his parish, as compared with those claimed by the local Christian Scientists. In making the study he enlisted the aid of the town physicians. Now he contends that his proportion of cures was larger than that claimed by the Scientists, and that this may be the case in any normal parish. The amazing conclusion was that the Scientists reported 95 per cent of their patients cured, and the Episcopalians 98 per cent.[4]

Days of convalescence afford the pastor a beautiful opportunity. He can tarry longer. He can take full advantage of the opening for evangelism or Christian nurture. If all seems to be well with the patient spiritually, there may be a call for humor, or other diversion, though never boisterous. In short, leave the friend with happy recollections of his pastor in the sickroom.

In another case things take a turn for the worse. The friend is rushed off to the hospital and is told to prepare for a major operation on the morrow. The poor fellow may know nothing about the ways of nurses and surgeons. He may associate the operating room with the lodge brother who died there a week ago. Who has time enough and knowledge sufficient to help the terror-stricken friend make ready for the oncoming shock? Surely the pastor should be prepared to render first aid, spiritually. He may refer to the skill of the surgeon. Better yet, the minister can lead his friend to rely on God.

One of the surest ways to help is to read slowly a favorite psalm, such as the One Hundred and Third, at least the first half. Then let there be a prayer, with a benediction. Before leaving the room, promise to pray for this friend tomorrow at the hour of the operation. If he wishes to see you then, ask the nurse if it will be convenient for you to be present. In any case, stand by him! The spiritual value of such ministrations depends much more on what you are than on what you say or do. By God's grace, cultivate a " healing presence."

The power of a healing presence appears in a novel about life in England during World War II. A retired general practically adopts a little slum cripple called Limpy. The wee fellow has suffered so much at the hands of so-called surgeons that he dreads the approaching operation. " O sir, I carn't fice it! I carn't, I tell you, I carn't! " " Hold on, old boy," says the General. " A few short weeks, and a little pain; that's all there is to it. Then you and I will kick a football over Farthing Knoll." That was the General's ancestral mansion. He too had been a cripple and had shown Limpy a leg all covered with scars left by the army surgeon's knife.

" In the presence of the doctors and nurses Limpy steeled himself never to utter a whimper. It was only when they two were alone together that the child clutched the old gentleman and piteously wept out his fears. The General was Limpy's safety valve. It had been a strain, a very great strain. At each successive scene the General had felt his own strength draining out of him. Well, it was all over now. Limpy would walk again."

When Limpy half apologized for hurting the General's feelings, the elderly gentleman replied: " Not making me feel bad, old chap. I like to be close to you and share your secret thoughts. You've put up a brave front, Limpy, with everyone else. Proud of you, my boy! " Thus the novelist shows the meaning of masculine sympathy. The General had previously taught the wee lad how to deal with his nickname: " The only way to take the sting out of a nickname is to accept it." In a skillful way that ought to be common among clergymen, the General at last induced timorous Limpy to walk. In short, this old warrior shows one how to hearten a terror-stricken patient, both before and after a surgical operation.[5]

4. The Case of Contagion. The minister does well to consult a kind physician about what to do in a case under quarantine. Some maladies are contagious: the disease is carried by contact with a sick person, or some object he has touched. The term " infectious disease " is broader. It includes such maladies as diphtheria, where the disease spreads through the saliva. The bacteria may travel through the air. Especially in talking with doctors and nurses, the pastor should be careful not to use such terms incorrectly. He should understand that there is far more danger of infection from a severe case of influenza than from pulmonary tuberculosis under proper control.

The pastor should take the same sort of precautions as the physician. To refuse to call where a doctor and a nurse are in attendance would be a proof that a minister does not trust God. On the other hand, he ought not to expose himself unduly. He should never carry contagion to children, including his own. In the sickroom let him avoid leaning over the patient. Unless there is need of doing so, he should not touch the patient or the bed clothes. Six feet from the patient's head should be close enough. But the clergyman should call no attention to the fact that he is standing aloof. Before leaving the house, if possible, let him wash his hands in a solution of mercuric chloride. This he can secure in tablet form and carry with him in a little vial. Let him be sure to empty and drain the wash bowl, as the drug is poisonous.[6]

In making up the list of afternoon calls, let this one be last. Tarry briefly. Then take a walk in the open air, facing the wind. On reaching home it may be wise to change clothes and leave the outer garments to air in the basement, or else outdoors. The linen should be washed by itself, and at once. However, these precautions prove needful only in cases such as smallpox, where the danger of contagion is acute. The person who most dreads such a disease is the one most likely to succumb. Take all reasonable precautions and then go forward in faith. God will take care of you when you do His will in His way.

5. The Things to Avoid. In visiting the sick, the minister should call no attention to himself. Starting with the patient where he is, one should lead him to think about God. Why need the pastor obtrude himself? He might do so by lack of neatness in dress or person; by failure to shave or clean his nails; by wearing soiled linen or a shabby coat; by having unpolished shoes or a frayed necktie; by failure to bathe or by offensive breath. If he must indulge in tobacco, let him do so in the privacy of his room at home. No sick friend, easily upset, should be exposed to offensive odors.

The tactful caller does nothing to irritate outworn nerves. He refrains from loud talking and laughing, shaking the bed or knocking against a chair, standing stiffly or moving jerkily, walking on tiptoe or roaring like a lion. Of course he ought to make himself heard if the friend proves to be deaf. Even so, the pastor's voice will sound more restful on its lower notes. If he has ever been ill at a hospital he knows that the beds are high and that the visitor needs to be stationed where he can easily be seen. Sometimes he should stand at the foot of the bed. If so, let him stay there, and keep his hands to himself. Experience will guide him away from errors, if he keeps his eyes open, and if he really cares, in the spirit of the Golden Rule.

The pastor ought to refrain from talking about himself and his pastoral calls. He should not carry news concerning his other sick friends, except occasionally to tell about those who are getting strong. He should beware against referring to his own aches and pains, or to his previous illnesses and operations. Rather should he go about as the apostle of health and as the bearer of good news. He can serve as a living example of the restfulness, the poise, and the hopefulness that Christ imparts to a trustful soul.

Even in the most critical cases the minister need not inform any patient that he is about to die. More than a few times the author has seen " dying " persons rally. Sometimes they recover. Dr. Louis Tucker narrates such an experience.[7] He was asked to notify a sick woman that her end was drawing near: " I balk at telling people they are dying. . . . I therefore told the lady that everything had been done for her that medicine could do. The outcome, now, was in the hands of God. Trust to Him. . . . She said that if everything were in God's hands she would not worry any more. Then she turned her face to the wall and went to sleep — and woke up, later, demanding gumbo soup."

During the present writer's boyhood his father was called out in consultation with two of the ablest surgeons in the community. The three medical men agreed that the twelve-year-old girl would die in agony unless her appendix was removed at once. Her parents flatly refused to put their darling under any man's knife. Within half an hour after the doctors had departed, shaking their heads solemnly, the abscess burst into the intestine. Later that day the girl was playing out on the street.

If her pastor had called during those critical thirty minutes before the abscess burst, he might have been asked to inform her that she was dying. If he had done so, she might have died of fright. But if not, he would have become the neighborhood laughingstock. If he had prayed over her and then promised a cure without resort to the knife, he might have been hailed as a miracle worker. As it was, nature took its course. Why should the minister guess? Why should he not leave all that to the doctor?

Last winter the author was asked to visit the local hospital and christen a " blue baby " girl. His heart went out to the parents, who had become reconciled to giving up their first-born child. They were told that the infant might live a few days or weeks, but that there was no hope of her becoming a healthy child. Today she is almost a year old and as well as any little one in town. Did the healing come because of that baptismal service? Who can tell? At any rate, the minister did not pronounce the committal service over the sleeping babe. Rather did he entrust her to the keeping of the Lord. The healing

power came from God, doubtless through the physicians who
had pronounced the case hopeless.

Such a case once or twice in a decade should not mislead the
pastor into distrust of the doctors. They are not inspired or infallible, but neither is he. The best medical men deserve to
wear the mantle of the divine Physician. They are willing to
work hand in hand with the minister who believes in the use of
God-given means for the restoration of health. Those means
include prayers for the sick. From any up-to-date physician or
surgeon the pastor can learn how to excel in the fine art of
ministering to sick friends, one after another. He will often
give thanks for the Christian doctor.

Sooner or later, illness will come to the pastor or his wife.
Once a minister preached about " Religion for Sickness and
Health." The sermon sounded almost like an echo of Mary
Baker Eddy. He felt secure because he had passed through two
epidemics of influenza and had buried a score of the friends on
whom he had called. The next day after that message he went
to bed with a high fever. Soon he developed pneumonia. Inci-
dentally, he learned not to boast about his ability to keep well.

A minister's illness may prove to be a means of grace. Not
until he suffered from serious sickness did Thomas Chalmers
begin to be a home-going pastor among a churchgoing people.[8]
If such an experience comes during the first few months of a
new pastorate, and if the affliction is accepted in humble trust,
that ministry is almost sure to be blessed. The people start
praying for their pastor, and he intercedes for them. Day after
day " by faith they meet around the common mercy-seat."
Throughout their later years together, the hearts of pastor and
people will be bound up in the fellowship of Christ's sufferings.

Why not learn how to excel in " the art of ministering to
the sick "? As a reward in this world you will find abundance
of joy. In the life hereafter you will hear the Master say: " Well
done, thou good and faithful servant." " I was sick, and ye
visited me."

Suggested Readings

Dicks, Russell L., *And Ye Visited Me*. Harper & Brothers, 1939.

Emerson, L. Eugene (ed.), *Physician and Patient*. Harvard University Press, 1929.

Frost, Evelyn, *Christian Healing*. Morehouse-Gorham Company, Inc., 1940.

Hiltner, Seward, *Religion and Health*. The Macmillan Company, 1943.

Robinson, George C., *The Patient as a Person*. Oxford University Press, London, 1939.

Wise, Carroll A., *Religion in Illness and Health*. Harper & Brothers, 1942.

XIII

The Plight of Shut-in Friends

THE most neglected folk in the parish may be the shut-in friends, especially the aged. In our time the Church has devoted itself largely to young people and children. This may be partly why the Church School has suffered a sad decline. God never intended the Bible School to be solely for boys and girls. Meanwhile the number and the proportion of elderly persons has been increasing annually.[1] Many of them feel neglected. Because of their infirmities and pains, some have become querulous. They can do little but brood. Hence they are ready to appreciate pastoral care. They are also quick to resent signs of " absent treatment." Others, however, make the minister feel uplifted after every call. How should he care for shut-in friends?

1. *The Plan for These Upper Rooms.* Be sure to treat all the shut-in sufferers alike. The pastor may slip in to see one dear old saint who does his soul good, and then steal past the shut-in sister who gives him the shivers. Before long the word will go out over the grapevine telephone that he seems " choosy." The dear old saint on whom he calls would forgive him if he remained away. The less perfect sister is sure to deplore the fact that he comes so seldom. Sometimes such criticism may be due to previous lack of discretion. That in turn may have arisen from his failure to plan wisely.

At first the incoming pastor may take excellent care of shut-in friends. He may fix on regular times of the month for these calls, and then keep to his schedule. Soon the most childish of the shut-in sisters will begin to boast: " My minister comes to see me the first Tuesday of every month, rain or shine." With the passing of the days his ardor may wane, or his other duties may increase. Soon the songs of the upper room will give way to sighing: " The mean thing has forgotten me! "

Why arouse extravagant expectations? Is the minister of the Gospel to be as predictable as the man who reads the gas meter? Why not arrange to give each of these friends a surprise visit whenever it accords best with the regular work? Let the calls assume all sorts of forms, with reference to time as well as tone color. For instance, stop to see a querulous sister after house-mothers have begun to make ready for the evening meal. Save up a joke or two. Read a little poem with a jolly jingle. Remember that the shut-in sister may desire attention rather than treatment. In short, use imagination, which means the Golden Rule in action.

2. *The Spirit of the Call.* These counsels have to do with the approach. What such folk usually need is religion. Some of them are already attuned to the Infinite. They want to hear more about God. Others may be believers whose piety needs to be replenished. In one of his last books the late John Buchan declared that it was fairly easy to be brave when one felt strong in body. On the other hand, Christian faith ought to impart the ability to say, " I can do all things through Christ." Did not the apostle learn how to make his " stake in the flesh " a means of blessing to himself and others?

Gently the loving minister can lead the querulous sister to " make friends with her infirmity." If he succeeds, he should win the gratitude of her family circle. The benefits of the treatment, however, may last only three or four weeks. Within each calendar month, if not slightly oftener, the personal representative of " love, joy, peace, longsuffering, kindness, goodness, faithfulness, meekness, self-control " should call with a fresh supply of transforming grace. Learn to excel in this kind of " faith cure."

Why do we assume that the shut-in friends must all be women? Whatever the reason, only one out of three or four may be a man. Among all these afflicted folk, however, one of the men may be the most wretched. What does a man know about being cooped up indoors by day, and being confined long hours to his bed? He has acquired no hobby that he can keep up now. He has won few friends who care enough to call. He may not be able to read long at a stretch. He does not know how to knit, and he does not wish to learn. He can listen to the radio, but he hates much that he hears. Thus he shows that he is not a moron. What does he need, under God, so much as a minister who loves him, without a semblance of pity?

The husky clergyman may find it hard to sympathize with a feeble old man. Like the younger members of the family circle, who neglect grandpa upstairs, the pastor prefers the company of the strong and the successful. He can show more tolerance for the foibles of a dear old lady than for the whims of a weak old man. Nevertheless, if the minister learns how to deal with such an elderly friend, both of them will become better Christians. Somehow the loving shepherd can help the shut-in sufferer see that God still cares for His worn-out servant. Gradually the minister should help this aged friend discover some quiet outlet for the available time and strength.

These loving ministries lead to one upper room after another. The work appears at its best on a certain Lord's Day when the pastor and one of the lay officers take the Communion to shut-in friends. The official board plans for such a special service on the day of the Lord's Supper in the sanctuary. If the Sacrament is celebrated every month, as it may well be, and at different hours of the Lord's Day, it might not seem wise to give communion to the same shut-in friends so frequently. The present discussion relates to what we used to term the quarterly Communion.

The pastor and his lay friend administer the Sacrament only where they have been invited. They do so on the afternoon of the high day in the sanctuary, so that the shut-in friends may feel sure that they still belong to " the great congregation." Through the church bulletin, a week in advance, the word goes forth that any shut-in friend who so desires may receive the Holy Communion on the coming Lord's Day, between three and five o'clock. On Communion Day the notice is repeated in the bulletin. The reason for waiting to be invited is

Communion

The Plight of Shut-in Friends 119

that the two representatives of the home church do not know
where such loving ministrations will be convenient. On any
particular afternoon the shut-in friend may not feel able for
this unusual privilege, however brief and simple the ceremony. But when the invitation arrives, as often it will, the
pastor and his lay brother should expect to enjoy a mountaintop experience.

Someday before long the word will come that a certain shut-
in friend has gone home to her God. In that hour will the pastor receive thanks for his previous faithfulness, or will he
suffer twinges of conscience? Has he been so busy here and
there that now he feels like a stranger in the upper room? Then
he may wonder why the " friends " telegraph to a former pastor, inviting him to speak words of farewell over the earthly
form of the aged one whom he has loved from afar.

In the light of the coming day when you will stand at the
grave of some shut-in sufferer, why not resolve to take proper
care of every friend now confined in an upper room?

Suggested Readings

Dicks, Russell L., _Meditations for the Sick_. Willett, Clark & Com-
    pany, 1937.
Jones, E. Stanley, _Abundant Living_. Abingdon-Cokesbury Press,
    1942.
Scully, Frank, _More Fun in Bed_. Simon and Schuster, Inc., 1934.
Speer, Robert E., _Five Minutes a Day_. The Westminster Press, 1943.

Organize shut-in's
into a prayer Band—
Pray for pastor + church
— helps church —

Blackwood : "The Funeral"

XIV

The Ministry to the Sorrowing

WHEN has our old world been so full of sorrow as now? Among all the throng at morning worship next Sunday morning, how many hearts will be free from grief and fear? How many will simply be existing from hour to hour, filled with all sorts of suspense? How many will spend the rest of their lives without the support of loved ones dearer than all else on earth? Whatever the other needs of the parish, nothing except soul-winning can be so vital as comfort for friends in sorrow.

Does every pastor know that the grief due to war lasts on through many years? Take a concrete example. During the War Between the States the eldest son of the Watterson family went away as a soldier. All at once he ceased to write home, and his loved ones could only surmise what had befallen their boy. Years later, long after the peace of Appomattox, they learned that he had been taken prisoner and that he had died at Andersonville. He had been the pride and joy of his mother's heart. During those years of suspense she contracted " shaking palsy." For a whole generation after the war she went to church every Sabbath Day. What did she wish most of all? Comfort! When her pastor went to the home, she wanted to hear about heaven, where her son dwelt with God.

1. *The Hope of Heaven.* In the days of that dear old saint the typical minister dealt much with heaven. To this Biblical truth we all should now return. According to beloved Bishop Edwin H. Hughes, " In these periods of stress the Church is the depository of comfort, and the minister its agent. The minister presides over the one altar to which the sorrowing can flee. . . . I am disturbed when I hear a minister indulge in a flippant contrast about being more interested in ' good tenements on earth than in many mansions in heaven.' Why set in opposition things that belong in one Gospel? It is simply dread-

ful to drop the eternal note. A Gospel for this world only is a tiny fragment, if Jesus spoke truly. Gibbon was right when he declared that one of the reasons for the spread of our faith was its glorious dogmatism about the eternal life." [1]

Elsewhere in a stirring autobiography Bishop Hughes calls for more of the burning heart in public worship, including the sermon. When people come to church today they need hymns and prayers full of Christian feeling. The same holds true in sorrow at home, when the pastor brings the consolations of God. As for the funeral service, the writer has dealt with that elsewhere.[2] The heart of the whole matter proves simple: except for evangelism, nothing in the minister's work these days ought to bulk so large as comfort. That means to strengthen hearts in God.

Sometimes at ministerial conferences we discuss two related " problems." Obviously we overwork this word problem, which does not appear in the New Testament. Nevertheless, the Holy Scriptures teach us to be on our guard against some tendencies. One problem has to do with the drifting away of our church members. The other relates to their joining certain cults, or " newer religions." For neither of those " problems " has any person found a cheap and easy solution. Even so, one dares to indulge in a sweeping generalization:

The defection usually springs from lack of pastoral care, especially in times of sickness and sorrow. Why are some congregations not affected by such falling away? Is it not because the minister mingles with the people day after day until he knows the needs of breaking hearts? Then on the Lord's Day the services in the sanctuary show the people how to get right with God even when they must walk through the valley of the shadow of death. As for the cults, instead of throwing stones, why do we not study their methods until we learn that heaven must bulk large in our religion during these days of war and rebuilding?

2. *The Kindness of the Shepherd.* How can a minister help friends who are passing through experiences he never has

one preacher — visits every home in
near community where death occurs
not to proselit + as act as a pastor
but as a friend

known? For one of various answers let him read *The Life and Letters of Phillips Brooks*.[3] How could that Boston clergyman — well, strong, and unmarried — enter into the spirit of Helen Keller, a blind girl ten years of age? At any rate, Brooks did so enter. He put himself in her place; he looked out on her little world as she should have looked; and thus he led her to God as Heavenly Father. In much the same fashion he must often have dealt with mature friends, one after another, when their eyes had been blinded by sorrow. In short, the pastor who wishes to excel as a comforter must know God and love people.

Such a kind shepherd needs to be sure what he believes. If he is like many an educated minister today, he can speak much more convincingly about the " nature of man " than about his " destiny." That seems to hold true even with Dr. Reinhold Niebuhr's strong Gifford Lectures.[4] The New Testament, on the other hand, deals far more fully with the destiny than with the nature. Why not rest content with recent erudite speculations about man's immortal soul, and take time to discover what the Saviour and His apostles teach about the resurrection of the body and the life everlasting? In these next few decades there should be a revival of study and teaching about Biblical eschatology. Then it will afford a basis for effective pastoral work. Be sure what you believe about the hereafter.

The plea here is for no particular variety of Christian doctrine. Naturally the writer accepts the creed of his Church, a creed conservative. However, he welcomes these words from the late Lyman Abbott, who counted himself a liberal: " I think of death as a glad awakening from this troubled sleep which we call life; as an emancipation from a world which, beautiful though it be, is still a land of captivity; as a graduation from this primary department into some higher rank in the hierarchy of learning.

" I think of the dead as possessing a more splendid equipment for a larger life of divine service than was possible to them on earth — a life in which I shall in due time join them if I am counted worthy of their fellowship in the life eternal.

Dont — Preach folks into Hell
tin funeral consign then to
Heaven.

"Do they know us, love us, hope for our coming? Shall we know them, love them, and may we hope for their fellowship? Surely! What is there left to be immortal in us if love and hope die? To exist without love and hope is not to live; to exist with hope always disappointed and love always denied would hardly be to live. What Scripture and philosophy alike promise us is life eternal, not eternal sleep; faith, hope, and love are the essentials of life." [5]

For such glad assurance turn often to the Bible, especially the parts that tell most about the Resurrection of our Lord. Listen to Henry Ward Beecher. The subject of his morning sermon on September 27, 1868, was "The God of Comfort." The text of that postwar discourse was II Cor. 1:3, 4. These were the opening words:

"I call the New Testament the Book of Joy. There is not in the world a book which is pervaded with such a spirit of exhilaration. Nowhere does it pour forth a melancholy strain. Often pathetic, it is never gloomy. Full of sorrow, it is full of victory over sorrow. In all the round of literature there is not another book that can cast such cheer and inspire such hope. Yet it eschews humor and foregoes wit. It is intensely earnest and yet full of quiet. It is profoundly solemn and yet there is not a strain of morbid feeling." [6]

Why did the strongest clergymen of yesterday excel in comforting the saints? Partly because those ministers lived and served during the awful days of 1861–1865, as well as afterward. Each of the pastors mentioned above — Brooks, Abbott, and Beecher — served throughout the War Between the States, and then lived on to comfort those that mourned. Such facts cause one to hope that World War II will lead a host of young clergymen to excel in binding up wounded hearts and in making them whole through the mercy of Christ.

Someone may ask, "How can I find time for all this ministry among the sick and the sorrowing?" Let him remember that these friends ought to have the priority. He may learn something about time-saving and system by reading the biog-

exact justice — not what we think he deserves.

Thy felt. "to his original own name"

Suicide: "appointed unto man once to die — after that the judgment

a possibility at closing minutes of life.

raphy of the late Frederick W. Farrar. As a contemporary of Phillips Brooks, Farrar belonged in the old Victorian days when nothing else on earth seemed so precious to a Christian pastor as the soul in sickness or in sorrow. At St. Margaret's in London, amid all his manifold labors, Farrar gave himself tirelessly to the sick and the sorrowing. There he had associated with him three curates, whom he guided in doing the routine parish work. But he declared that there was never a case of serious illness or sorrow to which he did not give personal attention. Who follows in his train?

a brief call immediatly after hear of death. have prayer. make no suggestions about funeral unless requested.

be prepared for any emergency.

To be interested is to
be accurate
— Sign in rectory

XV

Sermons - should
be filed - textualy
Cross-Red. topicah
Special days
Sepere note books
Easter
Christma
Mothersda
etc

The Habit of Keeping Records

THE dreariest part of pastoral work may consist in trying to keep adequate records. If a man were a practicing physician, or an army chaplain, he would have to endure still more of such drudgery. In time he ought to outgrow his feeling of distaste. As Dr. Louis Tucker writes about something else, "We loved our job so much that we soon enjoyed it." This principle holds true in all things pastoral. If a man is engaged in work appointed for him of God, he will enjoy whatever he does well, and he will do well whatever he enjoys. "The heart of man has an instinct for its real duties."

The entertaining book by Dr. Tucker stresses the importance of keeping records. Here are excerpts: "The growth of any Protestant congregation depends on the 'personality' of the minister, [and] on the excellence of his pastoral bookkeeping. . . . None of these things is taught in the seminaries. There is a course in pastoral theology, but it deals with grand matters, like converting atheists (there aren't any more; they are all agnostics!), and says nothing about practical matters like making lists of calls. . . . No seminary I ever heard of had a course in pastoral bookkeeping."

"What a parish needs is pastoral calling. Run, walk, crawl, die if you must, but visit!" [The rector tells how he once revived a "dead church."] "The membership growth had come from unrelenting pastoral calling. Such calling has to be by lists, or you go to see personal friends, and skip the uncongenial. Nor is calling enough. You have to study people, and say the right thing, or sit still and say nothing, which is harder." [1]

1. *The Extent of Such Records.*   The discussion here concerns what should go into the pastor's files. The question about

office records belongs under Church administration. In the study there should be an up-to-date list of all the members, with their addresses. These names usually appear on cards, by families, in alphabetical order. There should likewise be a list of the same persons according to streets, or other geographical districts. Every name that goes into the alphabetical file should also appear in the other. If the street is the ordinary district unit, one selects only the highways on which numbers of the people live. Then one groups with these persons the members who live near by. Thus there may evolve twelve or twenty " districts."

These lists the pastor may run through every week. One way to do so is to pray round the congregation on Saturday evening. There should also be a list of prospective members, for whom one often prays. After a man has visited his people for a few months, he should have almost as many " prospects " as there are names on the membership roll. Where is the congregation that has won to Christ more than half its ideal constituency? On the back of each card relating to a prospect, there may be certain hieroglyphics to guide in later visits by the pastor or some chosen worker.

If the minister conducts a pastor's hour, he will need a separate record for each person who comes. Such notes ought to be more detailed than anything described thus far. They should be kept under lock and key. The sexton may have a highly developed bump of inquisitiveness, as well as a ready tongue. What delicious morsels of gossip he could uncover by reading the minister's accounts of sins confessed! Not even the pastor's wife needs to know what such files contain. When the minister retires, or dies, the contents should be burned.

As for sermons, they can be filed topically or textually. The writer recommends the textual method. It encourages the use of the Bible in preaching, and the habit of choosing texts that glow. As for other addresses, they should be put away under topics. Those prepared for special occasions, such as talks at the Rotary Club, need to be filed under the names of the various organizations, alphabetically. If a man goes back to speak before the same group twelve months later, he wishes to know what he said and did the last time.

Important letters should be filed alphabetically, according to the family names of the writers. With each letter should go a carbon copy of the reply. If a man forms the habit of keeping such copies, he will be careful about what he sends forth. In a business communication, the less one writes the better. As for personal messages, they need not be held to such rigid limits. There is no business reason for keeping friendly epistles, or the replies.

Still another part of the records should contain the fruits of a man's reading. Since this does not usually relate to pastoral work, we shall not tarry long. However, if a minister forms the habit of reading books worth while, and if he preserves the best of what he reads, he can take at home a postgraduate course in pastoral theology, or almost any other subject. In order to become a skillful pastor, a young man ought to read much and that with care.

An accurate record of marriages performed may sometime prevent embarrassment. Twenty years after one leaves a certain parish, an attorney may ask for a certified statement about a particular ceremony. In the files one should have at hand the printed form supplied to the clergyman by the local Bureau of Vital Statistics. On that slip, before one performed the ceremony, one should have recorded the facts that may be asked for. Much the same kind of data ought to be kept about funerals and baptisms.

In addition to such files it is good to have in chronological order copies of the church bulletin or calendar. If these printed or mimeographed sheets have been well edited, they will provide materials enough for a spiritual history of the congregation. For instance, the bulletin ought to show how many people came to the Lord's Supper a week ago, or ten years before. Better still, these files ought to afford copies of any special services that may need to be reproduced in part.

Other uses for the files will suggest themselves. In fact, a man has to be on guard lest he become a bookkeeper instead of a pastor. As a minimum he should have at hand everything that will help him save time and energy. At the beginning of his career — preferably at the seminary — he can experiment. Gradually he should learn how to keep records without worry or waste of time. After a while there may be a church secretary, who can take care of the details, except those that should remain purely confidential. The secretary will be much more useful if the minister understands clearly what kind of records she ought to keep.

2. *The Mechanics of Keeping Records.* The author has discussed the matter elsewhere, as it concerns preaching.[2] Much the same ideas relate to pastoral work. One can use cards, preferably four by six inches. When purchased by the hundred, they are not costly. In preparing to make calls, it is easy to take out certain cards and put them in the pastor's notebook. This book he carries in his left side pocket. In selecting such a book he should secure one that will hold cards the size of those in his files.

For larger items, such as sermons, addresses, and letters, there should be Manila folders about ten by twelve inches. In pastoral work, however, nearly all the information can go on cards.

When the pastor moves into another parish, what should he do with these records? He may well leave his successor the lists of members. As for most of the other records, they should be kept. A hundred cards weigh only half a pound and fill only an inch of space in the files. At the next parsonage they can be put on a remote shelf, there to repose until needed.

The man with the shepherd heart does not flit about from field to field. In fact, the home-going pastor may not move often enough for his own good, and that of the flock. A man's first pastorate may continue six or eight years. After that he may think in terms of ten years. Among the Churches the writer has known, the pastorates that have continued much beyond ten years have usually proved anticlimactic. However, there have been various noteworthy exceptions. Most men move too much.

On the way to visit a former charge a glance over the right sort of records ought to prove helpful. Of course a kind minis-ter does not return to a former field unless the invitation comes from his successor. Even then, such visits ought not to be nu-merous, especially during the first few years of separation. Whatever the occasion that calls one back, the records from past years will provide facts that should enter into the picture. For instance, the pulpit may be vacant. If one goes to the for-mer parish for a funeral, one will wish to know something about the other funerals one conducted in the same family circle. A glance over the appropriate cards ought to bring out this information.

Two words of caution may be in order. First, never let a layman see such records. Like the physician's notes about his cases, the pastor's bookkeeping should concern no one but him-self. However, he can make an exception in favor of the friend who helps in the office. If she cannot keep all sorts of secrets, she ought not to become the church secretary.

Again, let the minister never use these records as a basis for boasting. Not even in a farewell sermon should this sort of self-glory prove needful. Why recount the number of calls he has made and his other numerical achievements? Whether or not the dear man means to boast, he should have something more worthy of such a vital occasion. " No man can bear witness to Christ and to himself at the same time." In a farewell sermon why not dwell more largely on the book of The Acts, with its message of divine power, than in the book of Numbers, with its human statistics?

In short, be a good craftsman. " Study to shew thyself ap-proved unto God, a workman that needeth not to be ashamed " (II Tim. 2:15).

Suggested Readings

Blackwood, Andrew W., *The Funeral*, Ch. XVIII, " The Permanent Records." The Westminster Press, 1942.
Cashman, Robert W., *The Business Administration of a Church*. Willett, Clark & Company, 1937.

Other Kinds of Pastoral Work

PART TWO

Other Kinds of Factory Work

XVI

The Usefulness of a Kit Bag

ONE of the most suggestive chapters in Cabot and Dicks' *The Art of Ministering to the Sick* bears the title "The Minister's Kit-Bag." The idea is to leave with the convalescent patient, or shut-in friend, something interesting, not exciting, to relieve the tedium of lonely hours. Such a gift or loan ought to be unexpected and lasting. Flowers have sweet uses, but that sort of present comes from the women of the church. The pastor also wishes to leave some visible reminder of his concern. The value of the token depends more on its appeal than on its cost. What interests and helps one friend would bore or annoy another. The use of a kit bag calls for a little money and much imagination.

1. *The Variety of the Contents.* The term "Kit-Bag" must be figurative. Nothing less than a huge box would hold such a diverse collection as the one listed here. Let us begin with books. For use in the sickroom a volume should be light in weight. The printing ought to be in large type, on paper without a glare. The choice of reading matter should depend on the taste of the invalid. For a little girl one might select a book of nonsensical verse by A. A. Milne, such as *Winnie-the-Pooh,* or *When We Were Very Young.* For a lad somewhat older, who is thinking much about preparatory school, one could take *Tom Brown's School-Days,* by Thomas Hughes. A woman naturally jolly might enjoy *Our Hearts Were Young and Gay,* by Cornelia Otis Skinner and Emily Kimbrough.

A strong man, if scholarly, ought to relish one of John Buchan's romances, such as *Prester John,* or *Mountain Meadow.* However, the latter might seem long for an invalid. A woman of different interests would appreciate a book about Madame Chiang Kai-shek, Sir James M. Barrie's account of his mother.

Margaret Ogilvy, or a volume of poems by Emily Dickinson. After the sick friend is able to read consecutively, she may enjoy the life of Mary Slessor, or Christina Forsyth, each by W. P. Livingstone. As in other fields of writing, the ablest works in biography do not come hot from the press.

A friend of a different sort would welcome a picture. Here again the field is broad. A biographer relates that in early years Cardinal Manning vainly strove to reach the heart of a dying shepherd. One day the clergyman brought a picture of the Good Shepherd. When the minister was making ready to leave, the old man whispered, " Don't take it away! " A few days afterward he died, without any sign of concern about his soul. However, the friends who prepared the body for burial found lying next to the heart that picture of the Good Shepherd.

Sometimes it is good to leave a copy of a poem or a hymn. If so, the printing ought to be on a card fairly stiff, so as to stand up under daily use. In the history of Protestantism the most famous pastor may have been Jean F. Oberlin, of the Vosges in France. At his home he had a printing press. Hence he could carry with him cards with all sorts of messages from the Bible. These he would leave with the friends on whom he called. Naturally the value of the plan depends in part on the selection of the poem, or Scripture verse, and on choosing the right card for each person. For an elderly man of " culture " the poem might be a portion of Browning's " Rabbi Ben Ezra." Whatever the selection, it should not be gloomy.

A more practical friend might prefer a mechanical puzzle, if not too tantalizing. A boy of this type would appreciate a gift of sea shells. In Asheville, N. C., the leading Episcopal rector takes his annual vacation in midwinter. He hies down to Florida and collects all sorts of sea shells. These he gives to sick boys in need of cheer. If the lad suffers a later illness, the clergyman brings shells to supplement the first assortment. Because of this hobby the clergyman is invited to lecture at large summer assemblies. He ought to feel still more highly honored because of his influence over boys at home. When he is in sight no one else can catch the attention of any lad to whom the rector has brought a gift of sea shells with all their varied splendor.

In our own parish the minister's wife keeps a "Treasure Chest." Really it is a tall cupboard with two tiers of shelves, one for little boys, the other for wee girls. Whenever a young lad goes to the manse on an errand he is led to the treasure chest. There he knocks and exclaims, "Boy!" Open flies the proper door. Then he can choose anything in sight, but only a single prize. Sometimes the invitation is sent out for a little girl to stop by at the manse. She too goes through mystic rites that lead to her bearing away some visible token of love that fills the hearts of her friends at the manse.

Into the replenishing of that treasure chest must go time and care, as well as imagination. Without knowing the facts, one dares to surmise that the custodian of the treasure chest keeps some sort of careful record. Otherwise when the little girls got together one of them might boast that she had been there twice. Then another would exclaim that she had never seen the storehouse full of mystic treasures. Fortunately, such mischances seem never to occur. Rather do fond parents wonder how the mistress of the manse keeps track of her adopted darlings, as well as her host of older friends.

2. *The Replenishing of the Kit Bag.* The problem of keeping the kit bag supplied may not prove so difficult as one would suppose. The minister does not go about scattering tokens broadcast like samples of breakfast food. Rather does he make such a gift occasionally, when least expected. If the book costs much, he may lend it for a week or two. However, if there seems to be need of an outright present, he does not hold back, whatever the cost. When our Lord bids us seek first the Kingdom, does He not make the promise, "All these things shall be added unto you"? He stands ready to provide everything needful for pastoral work.

Such a gracious supply may come through a godly woman. She may have ample means and a willing heart. She can likewise enlist her friends. It may be that the Women's Guild has a Pastor's Fund. If so, the matter should be kept secret. The gifts from the kit bag ought to come from the clergyman, in the name of the congregation. Thus the people will think of him in terms of the text, " God loves a man who is glad to give " (II Cor. 9:7, Goodspeed's Translation).

The value of the kit bag depends largely on the zeal and the tact of the minister. Does he really care for the friend slowly recovering from the first real sickness in sixty years? Does the pastor's heart go out to the shut-in sister whose rheumatic hands must often lie idle? Does he wish every solitary sufferer to have near by a visible token of the invisible grace that binds Christian hearts together at the mercy seat? If so, the Lord will guide His servant in the use of the proper ways and means. " If any man willeth to do his will, he shall know."

Suggested Reading

Cabot, R. C., and Dicks, R. L., *The Art of Ministering to the Sick,* Ch. XI, " The Minister's Kit-Bag." The Macmillan Company, 1936.

XVII

The Help of the Mail Carrier

WORLD WAR II has taught many a pastor to rely largely on the mail. Once a month an attractive newssheet has gone out to the ends of the earth. At their best these little magazines have shown editorial skill. Without seeming dull, some of the items have been distinctly religious. Chief among them has been a letter from the minister. Meanwhile he and others in the congregation have written countless personal messages. No feature of parish life has done more to make our young people feel enthusiastic about the home church and its leader. He in turn has found a new incentive for becoming a diligent pastor. At present we are to think about his use of the mail to reach friends in the parish.

1. The Variety of Uses. The following suggestions have to do with a congregation of average size, or larger. In a small church some of the proposals would scarcely prove feasible. There can be no counsel regarding church publicity or the raising of money. All of that has its place, but scarcely in the hands of the minister. Rather should he help to dispel a feeling that has grown all too common. Rightly or wrongly people say: " The only callers from our church come after money. The letters from our minister ask for more money." One way to silence these complaints is to promote the right sort of calling; another is to send out sprightly messages that do not concern finance.

It would be easy to overdo the writing of " form letters." Many of them are never read. Others induce a feeling of nausea. Occasionally, however, the right sort of congregational letter can do much good. At the beginning of the harvest season that culminates at Easter, a pastoral message tells the people what the official board has in view. Such a communication

ought to be printed, or at least mimeographed, on paper worthy
to represent the Church of Christ. The statement calls for first-
class postage. Needless to say, there should be no errors or slips
in spelling or typing. Let the home church be as well represented on paper as any community bank.

A more personal message may go out to the congregation.
After a year in which the goodness of the people has culmi-
nated at the Christmas season, the pastor and his wife may send
cards before New Year's Day. If these missives went out prior
to Christmas, they might become swamped in the holiday mail.
Before New Year's comes a lull. A card planned with loving
care will meet with a joyous welcome. It may show a " pen-
and-ink sketch " of the home church. There may be a snow
scene, with the sanctuary as it appears from a window in the
manse. Whatever the picture and the message, the card ought
to be signed by the minister and his wife. Then it will be kept
on many a piano.

As a rule pastoral letters and notes ought to be somewhat
personal. After the minister and his wife have been entertained
in a home, within a few days one of them ought to send the
hostess a " thank-you note." That may seem obvious. Perhaps
so, but not one hostess in a score receives such a token of appreciation on the part of her pastor. With our customary crude-
ness we clergymen accept costly courtesies as a matter of
course. Here the author is remembering his former sins and
charging them on his readers. He is glad to report, however,
that more recently his ministerial friends have learned better
manners. If a pastor voices his thanks aright, the daughter of
Martha will rejoice; if he also sends a worthy note, she will be
doubly glad.

Letters distinctly pastoral ought to prove still more rewarding. The next few paragraphs owe much to a little book by
Dr. B. C. Clausen, who has recently gone from Pittsburgh to
Cleveland. On the birthday of each child in the Church School
he sends a special card, which he writes with ink. Somehow he

" dares " the recipient to respond by speaking to the minister after church the next Sunday morning. Among those who get such greetings, there is practically a hundred-per-cent response in the way of church attendance, at least for that Sunday. Afterward, doubtless, these young friends come often to the house of God.

Every baby born into a home of the parish likewise receives a special card. It is addressed to the infant at the hospital. Thus the first mail a newborn child receives is from the pastor. The church secretary keeps him supplied with the facts. She watches the newspapers with an eagle eye. Probably she does everything but sign those cards. Even so, the minister is able to visit the baby by mail before he could do so in person.

With an adult friend the pastor is likely to use a letter. Whenever any member of the parish has graduated from college, or has won a prize in athletics, the minister writes a brief note of felicitation. Such a message ought to go out at once. Belated congratulations might seem stale. So does the minister supplement his sick calls by sending letters. This method works also with shut-in friends, and those in sorrow. The difficulty is to compose a message worthy to be kept for months and years. Form letters will not do.

Even more unique is the message of welcome to each minister who comes to town. A similar greeting goes forth to every prominent newcomer, such as the superintendent of schools, or to any city official who has done a piece of work that deserves the thanks of church people. These messages appear not to suggest attendance at Dr. Clausen's church, though that might be the result. Ideally, they should help to tone up the civic life.

Still more gratifying is the following: " No official retires from service on our church boards, no soloist does particularly well on Sunday, no Sunday School teacher brings a group of boys and girls to be baptized, no important committee chairman is discharged after performance of duty, without a cor-dial, personal, handwritten letter from me, as soon after the event as possible." [1] Is it any wonder that Dr. Clausen terms the mail carrier an assistant pastor?

In Baltimore the late Maltbie D. Babcock used letters differently. With irresistible charm he made people glad by innumerable calls. He is said to have entered as many as twenty-five houses in a single day. For another man such a pace would not prove feasible. But the most fleeting glimpse of Babcock's face seems to have wrought wonders in the homes of God's people. At each place he would tarry only long enough to convey greetings and find out what he needed to know. Later in the day, or the night, perhaps when he should have been asleep, he would indite a note to each family he had visited since morning. Doubtless some of those messages are still preserved by friends whom he helped through the mail.

2. *The Wisdom of Writing Such Letters.*   Every minister can work out his own methods. The suggestion here is that a man use brief messages to supplement pastoral calling. The advantages should be obvious. The plan enables him to find the family at home, when they have time to spare. The right sort of note or letter shows that the minister cares. He personally receives so much mail that he may forget the situation among the humble folk in the parish. To many a faithful church member the coming of a brief note, written in ink and signed by the most beloved man in town, may constitute an event.

All the while one must be careful. To the following rule there can seldom be an exception: Whenever you have anything to say that may hurt the other person, go to him and speak face to face, in the spirit of love. Never put on paper what might not be displayed on the mantel. Whenever you have anything pleasing to communicate, write it down and send it by mail. Even if the friend lives round the corner, the right sort of note from the pastor will bring him abiding joy.

Writing such messages ought to become a matter of habit. If only one goes out each day, on the average, five days in the week, that means over two hundred and fifty letters a year.

Even when on a summer vacation, it should not prove wearisome to send a picture post card to every shut-in friend back at home. With the card should go a word of greeting, and a silent prayer. Some of these days that shut-in sister will bid farewell to earth. In her hands she will hold a loving note from " the dominie." Then the minister will be glad that he helped to brighten her long lonely hours in an upper room.

3. *The Difficulties About the Proposal.* With all his elaborate program for using the mails, Dr. Clausen estimates the cost at only $200 a year. For the average pastor, however, that sum seems prohibitive. So would the city minister's program be unsuitable in a typical parish. At first the pastor should work on a limited scale. Instead of faring forth in his automobile on a wintry day when the streets are an endless glare of ice, he can tarry at home and write briefly to the friends he would have seen that day. The stamps will cost far less than the repairs on a damaged automobile, or the setting of a broken leg.

In a church of any size the lay officials may sense the need of an office and a secretary. In the annual budget even the most conservative businessmen will gladly put a sum sufficient to cover the cost of the pastor's correspondence, except his personal letters. Those laymen are not hardheaded, but largehearted. For that very reason they do not wish to waste the Lord's money. When they learn that by use of the mail their pastor almost doubles his helpfulness in the community, they will thank God for such a minister. Not only does he call in person. He also expresses himself through writing. In this way John Calvin is said to have sent out four thousand letters, most of them pastoral. In them he showed a heart tender and warm.

At first glance the expenditure of time seems formidable. Here again, one must use common sense. It would not be wise to keep bombarding the same people with letters and notes. Such missives might seem like missiles. Any " pastoral epistle " ought to be an event, not an incident. Before one sits down to write, there ought to be a reason. When one has nothing to say, one says it, but not through the mail, or even the pulpit.

The plea here is not for a host of hasty effusions, but for a limited number of loving messages. Each of them ought to come from the heart. As a rule they ought to be short. They should be written by hand, not dictated to a stenographer and signed by proxy.

Every minister ought to master the art of writing brief messages. This daily exercise will help him to prepare to preach and pray. Into every note he should put a good deal of charm. On the other hand, if he says much the same thing time after time, he will discover that the good women get together and " compare notes." Even " thank-you " missives receive such scrutiny. But if a brief message comes from a heart full of love for God and His people, the note may be preserved for years as a household treasure.

If any minister desires to test the difference between the spoken word of appreciation and the written note of thanks, let him search his own heart. Last Sunday more than a few people thanked him for the morning service. Two said nothing as they clasped his hand. That night each of them sat down to compose a brief letter of thanks. He may already have forgotten the honeyed words of appreciation, but he carries those two notes about in his pocket. If they had been composed by an angel in heaven, they could scarcely have seemed more precious.

A recent experience will show how the principle works in a kind of " larger parish." No small portion of a chaplain's work overseas has consisted in writing letters of comfort to the loved ones of a stricken soldier or sailor. Such a message came from the Solomon Islands to a home in Louisville. The friends knew that their son's body had been rescued from the water and buried on an island the name of which they could only surmise. This letter the home pastor borrowed and read to his people on Memorial Sunday, when the congregation honored all the members who had gone home to God during the preceding year.

The same " ministering shepherd " afterward wrote a letter

of appreciation to the father of the chaplain. All the parties concerned were practically strangers to each other. Now they feel like intimate friends. Can anyone suggest how the chaplain overseas and the pastor in Louisville could have shown kindness more lovingly than by such use of the mail? Of course each of them showed judgment in what he wrote. Otherwise, a minister's letters might do more harm than good. Many of us write too much. Our epistles would be twice as effective if half as long. In composing a message of comfort, as in preparing a sermon, the following holds true:

" Three fourths of writing well consists in giving definite, well-chosen facts, and plenty of them. The other fourth doesn't matter." [2] That may sound extreme. If so, squeeze out the surplus. In view of what remains, the pastor should think of his pen as a means of grace. Of all the things in the study, apart from the Bible and the hymnbook, what can prove so helpful? Why not dedicate your pen to God in a definite act of prayer?

writing to soldiers - if change pastorate during war. - last letter - tell them - you are leaving + new pastor will take over.
If they keep writing, you might answer.

XVIII

The Blessing on a New House

UNTIL recent years some of us never had thought of blessing a new house. By this term one means an abode into which a Christian family has moved to establish a home. The structure itself may have been used by others, but as a rule it has come fresh from the hands of the contractor and the painters. Much the same principle may apply to another building. Recently our local pastor dedicated to the service of God a new edifice in which a long-established dry-goods firm proposed to start business afresh.

Needless to tell, the whole idea will appeal only to pastors and people who enjoy a degree of ceremony. With other strong churchmen it would be easy to start an argument. That is remote from the purpose here. The idea is rather to report facts. Some of our clergymen have adopted this custom with gratifying results. Especially for use among the Methodists, the Rev. Dr. E. A. Hunter, of Wichita Falls, Texas, has had printed a beautiful " Certificate of Dedication." The design embodies letters of blue on a background of gold, all in a form large enough for framing — eleven by thirteen inches. The most striking feature is the picture of an attractive home built on the Holy Bible. That is what every pastor longs to see throughout the congregation.

The home built on the Book! The undergirding idea is that both people and place belong to the Heavenly Father. Those who dwell in the house look on themselves as His stewards or trustees. Hence they invite the minister and one or two of the local church officers to set the place apart for the service of the Kingdom. For those who live there, the place in view ought to become the house of God and the gate of heaven. Here follows the wording on that " Certificate of Dedication ":

" In the name of God the Father Almighty, and of Jesus Christ His Son, and of the Holy Spirit, the Home of
has been dedicated to the deep affection of the family circle, to courage, patience, and self-control, to all beautiful things of the heart and mind, to Almighty God, the Christian faith, and the brotherhood of all mankind." Then a separate line invokes " reverence for these ideals on the part of all who share its hospitality." In many a household such a visible reminder of its God-given purpose should help to promote family religion. However, the idea of dedication involves much more than an attractive certificate to be framed and hung on the wall of the dining room.

1. *The Preparation Through Preaching.* The minister can introduce the custom by delivering a special sermon, perhaps on Mother's Day. Instead of concocting a conventional discourse, sentimental and even mushy, he may preach about " Religion in the Home." The text may be Deut. 6:4–9, which the present writer terms " The Hebrew Creed." For a rural parish the other version of the " Creed " may seem preferable. This alternate form appears in Deut. 11:13–21.

In Deut. 6:4–9 the opening words present the religion of the father. He ought to be the head of the household, just as the mother should be the heart of the home. For such an ideal of the father's leadership in household religion, turn to the autobiography of John G. Paton, the missionary to the New Hebrides.

The central portion of our Scripture deals with the religious training of children. According to the Bible, such nurture ought to be the chief concern of the Christian home. Saint Augustine used to say that when the Master spoke about two persons meeting together for prayer, He referred to husband and wife. When He alluded to three, He had in mind these young parents and their first-born babe. In the religious training of the child, and the little ones that will come later, the father should take the lead.

The closing portion of our " Hebrew Creed " stresses the use of religious symbols in the home. Thus the appeal comes to boys and girls chiefly through " eye-gate." In school these days, and almost everywhere else, they learn mainly through what they see. Why should it not be so with religion in the home? Such at least was the Hebrew conception of religious nurture. The gateway bore an inscription that meant, in substance: " This house belongs to God." On the doorpost stood a cylinder that contained " the mezuza," or " Hebrew Creed." Thus the Hebrew home, ideally, could have been called " God's Providence House."

How is it in the homes the pastor visits today? Do these places look Christian or pagan? It is said that Dr. G. Campbell Morgan visited one of his ministerial sons who had married and moved into a new parsonage. The young folk were delighted with their home. As they showed the father one room after another they noticed that he said nothing. When at last they asked why he kept silent, he replied: " The house is beautiful, but from cellar to garret there is nothing to show that it belongs to God." Sometimes it is so even in a parsonage today.

When visitors depart from beneath the roof, " what have they seen in thy house? " Why should there not be a copy of the Bible on the living-room table, with a hymnal on the piano? Should there not be religious books and magazines? Is there no place for religious pictures? Of course there should be grace at meals, and family prayers following, or at some other convenient time, both morning and evening. In short, as Bushnell says,[1] Christian parents should " bathe the child in their own feeling of love to God and dependence on Him." Throughout the home they should " make what is good [seem] happy and attractive; what is wrong, odious and hateful." Such are the ideals that lead to the service of dedication.

2. *The Plan for the Service.* The ceremony is likely to assume one of two forms. The first is short, and apparently unstudied. The other is more nearly elaborate and lasts slightly longer than a marriage service. The discerning pastor will know

which kind of service to conduct in any particular home. The present discussion has to do with a formal ceremony, since the other resembles a pastoral call.

The first occasion of the sort requires careful preparation. Unless the denominational book of worship contains such a ritual,[2] the pastor may need to make one of his own. From time to time he can employ much the same ceremony. At least one of the prayers, however, may deal with the interests of the home now being dedicated to the service of God. Better still, each of the prayers may concern the interests of the friends who dwell beneath the roof. As for the other parts of the service, there need be little change from time to time.

The ceremony ought to include brief passages of Scripture and short prayers. If the minister or the lay officer can start a familiar tune without an instrument, there may be portions of one or two old-time hymns. There need be little or nothing in the way of exhortation or rebuke. From God's Holy Book His servant can bring out every needed truth. Especially in Deuteronomy he can find the will of the Lord concerning household religion. In prayer he should lead every heart close to the God who loves to dwell in a Christian home. In short, let him make every part of the service uplifting.

The exercises ought to start at a given hour. It may be eight thirty on the first Monday evening in June. The members of the family circle ought to be present ahead of time. With them may be their close relatives and friends. There need be no refreshments or other semblance of an evening party. With the pastor may stand one or two lay officers of the home church, preferably those whose presence will mean much to the host and hostess. At least there ought to be one lay representative of the congregation, who should have been chosen by the official board. Both he and the minister ought to be attired as for a noteworthy occasion in the sanctuary. If local custom allows, the clergyman may don his pulpit gown, with the colored hood.

A young pastor in North Jersey expects soon to be married. Then he and his bride will move into a manse newly built.

They have been looking forward to an " open house," with an evening of social enjoyment and light refreshments. Now he asks how to combine these festivities with a semipublic ceremony of blessing the house that belongs to God's people. The obvious reply is that the ceremony should follow the informal gathering. At a stated hour, perhaps nine thirty, the ministerial guest of honor can summon the people together for a surprise. After any announcement that seems necessary, he can lead the assembled throng in setting apart this home for the service of God and the community. Such a ceremony may lead up to the singing of the Doxology, and the Benediction of Peace (Heb. 13:20, 21), all to be led by the visiting brother. If the service goes well, other families will wish to do what the pastor has done with " his " new house.

3. *The Ceremony of Dedication.* The following description concerns what we have been calling a typical home. The formal exercises start in the hallway. There the pastor sounds a call to worship, and reads one of the above-mentioned passages from Deuteronomy. Then he offers a brief invocation, including a short confession of sins. Before he goes into the adjoining room he requests those present to follow him and his lay friend. Afterward there need be no announcement. If the layman is gifted in public address he may lead at a certain stage. Of course he should have had abundant opportunity to prepare in advance. Then he will speak briefly.

In the living room the pastor repeats part of a hymn, such as " Now Thank We All Our God." In the dining room he reads about the giving of the manna, or the feeding of the five thousand. Then he offers a brief prayer of thanksgiving for God's loving care. If the people sing well without an instrument, he can lead them in a stanza of " Break Thou the Bread of Life."

Out in the kitchen the Biblical portion may be Zech. 14:20, 21, followed by a poem about " the God of pots and pans." Among the oldest and sweetest of such verses are those of " The Elixir," by George Herbert. There he sings, in part:

> " Teach me, my God and King,
> In all things Thee to see;
> And what I do in anything,
> To do it as for Thee.
>
> . . . .
>
> " A servant with this clause,
> Makes drudgery divine;
> Who sweeps a room as for Thy laws,
> Makes that, and the action, fine."

On the upper floor one need not go into every room. If there is a spacious landing at the top of the stairway, that will serve every need. In a home blessed with little children, simply read the One Hundred and Twenty-seventh and the One Hundred and Twenty-eighth Psalms. These two ancient songs tell about the security of the city in terms of the godly home. Still another psalm, for days of upheaval, would be the Forty-sixth, or the Ninety-first. The pastor may feel led to use the One Hundred and Twenty-first Psalm, which, with its reference to sleep, would lead up to the closing prayer.

This " pastoral prayer " ought to be the best of all, except the benediction. Without letting it grow long, one can commit to God's loving care each member of the household, and every interest dear to these hearts. If anyone in the family circle has begun to grow old, or if a son in the service has given up his life, the petitions may have much to do with the last long sleep which men call death. Under different conditions the climactic element would come in petitions for peace on earth and good will among men.

After this prayer those present should join hands while they repeat with the minister the Lord's Prayer. Still clasping hands, they should all sing a stanza of " Blest Be the Tie That Binds." Then the service of dedication closes with the Benediction of Light (Num. 6:24–26). In the spirit of these blessed words the pastor and his friends should say good night. He ought to depart in the glad assurance that the manifold blessings of the Triune God will abide in the home that has been set apart for the service of Christ as King.

Suggested Readings

Bailey, Albert E., *The Arts and Religion*. The Macmillan Company,
1944.
Stafford, Thomas A., *Christian Symbolism in the Evangelical
Churches*. Abingdon-Cokesbury Press, 1942.

whatever called upm to dedicate;
make it impressive —
is its' worth dedicating — do a good
do bo s it.

no set form — great variety

XIX

The Concern About Newcomers

"Our church is going back. More and more of our people are moving away. How can we hold our own? " Often one hears such a complaint. Sometimes the drift starts almost overnight. A factory closes and the workmen scatter. The moving van seems to be in constant demand. During the writer's last pastorate the loss by removals, geographically, averaged about a hundred members a year. In that field, as Alice would say in Wonderland, we had to keep moving forward so as not to slip back. " You see, it takes all the running you can do, to keep in the same place."

The problem became doubly acute during the early days of the war. From most congregations there was an exodus. Into centers of manufacturing there was an influx. Our hearts still go out to congregations that have lost some of their best families. At Washington, D. C., the Government statisticians tell us that with the coming of peace at least forty per cent of the people who have recently moved to engage in defense work will not return to their former homes. How can the local church attract such newcomers?

1. *The Importance of Early Contacts.* The best time to win a new family comes at once. In a strange neighborhood the newcomers ought to get their bearings, religiously, before the first Lord's Day. After that, every passing hour lessens the likelihood of their becoming attached to the local church. In a place new and strange the tender plant of household piety must struggle like a root growing out of dry ground. Transplanting imperils the life of a shrub or a tree. This may be why people hesitate to transfer their church letters. You would think they were talking about transplanting oak trees!

In terms of gardening, the pastor needs to be adept in transplanting. If one moves a shrub aright just before a rain, the

bush will almost surely thrive. If it must struggle through a
time of drought, the shrub will likely die. In other words, newcomers need neighbors and friends. If everyone in the vicinity
greets them with a stony stare, the new folk feel that the place
is God-forsaken. Even though they attend divine services,
they may become church tramps. Erelong the vagrants grow
weary of visiting unfriendly churches, and start staying at
home. Such experiences are common. They help to account for
our staggering " losses by removal."

The minister and the church secretary in the former parish
could help the newcomers to find their way into the local sanctuary. Instead of referring to their coming habitation as more
or less " God-forsaken," the former pastor can say with the
seer of old: " Seek the peace of the city whither I have caused
you to be carried away captives, and pray unto the Lord for
it: for in the peace thereof shall ye have peace." Once again:
" Build ye houses, and dwell in them; and plant gardens, and
eat the fruit of them " (Jer. 29:7, 5). In other words: " Start
a real home at once. Get the family roots imbedded in the
strange soil. Begin attending church the very first Sunday."

Such a practical philosophy concerns church letters. It never
seems wise for the minister to suggest that a certain family
" leave the home church." In general, however, he can promote the habit of taking certificates of membership to the new
community and depositing them at once with the " new "
church. In a certain congregation, whenever the minister is
about to welcome new members publicly, first he announces
the names of those who have been " certified to other churches."
Then he says, " If any family in the congregation moves beyond its bounds, we strongly advise them to take their church
letters and join the local church the first Sunday morning."
The home pastor can help still more by sending the " new "
minister the names and the address of the incoming household,
with any other pertinent facts. Such a present-day applica-
tion of the Golden Rule will help the pastor of the " new
church " to render " first aid."

Meanwhile that phrase " losses by removal " may cover a multitude of sins. Most of them seem to be sins of omission. We ministers appear to be the chief culprits. Our motto often seems to be: " Inasmuch as ye did it not." These words of our Lord about the Judgment Day have to do with being kind to strangers (Matt. 25:31–46). And yet our laymen wonder why certain congregations do not grow! The minister announces the names of boys and girls who join the Church. At the end of the year, if the books are correct, the total number of members may be no larger than at the beginning. The average attendance has been decreasing. " You see, it takes all the running you can do, to keep in the same place." Without having any actual proofs, one feels confident that such conditions usually obtain where there is a lack of pastoral work and lay visiting.

In a wide-awake church the opposite often holds true. Without neglecting any shrub that is firmly rooted and able to withstand a drought, the gardener watches over every plant that has recently been moved. While the minister himself may not perform the labor involved, he ought to be sure that it is done, the sooner the better. In gaining the good will of people who have just bidden farewell to the moving van, " time is of the essence of the contract." Let us therefore look at this matter more closely. The viewpoint throughout will be that of the " new " church and minister.

2. *The Winning of Newcomers.* In an urban community church people often have difficulty in learning about newcomers at once. In a certain congregation one of the men on the official board is head of a real estate agency. Through the gas company and the telephone office he gets the names of practically all newcomers. These he reports immediately to the church secretary. Other congregations rely largely on " the block method." Their district workers know the various parts of the community as intimately as mail carriers know their beats. Whenever a new family moves into the neighborhood, a representative of the congregation extends a welcome. Usu-

ally the church worker is a woman. If there is need of further attention she reports to the church office at once.

The pastor may tarry a day or two before he calls. Meanwhile the women of the district ought to have shown the newcomers the sort of attention that strangers like. At first they do not need callers so much as neighbors. With the offer to help in any way, perhaps with something hot to eat, there should come an invitation to attend church next Sunday morning. When the newcomers accept, they should go with pleasant anticipations: " These people know how to be friendly without seeming effusive. They have shown us kindness in a place where we expected coldness."

The worthy pastor knows how to show newcomers the loving-kindness of the Lord. Tactfully he learns what he should know about the various members of the household, including those away from home. He also finds out which parts of the church program appeal to the various members of the household. Somehow or other he keeps in touch with the new family until he feels certain that the transplanted shrub will thrive. All the while such a program may call for a change of attitude on the part of the local church. Do the members really want newcomers? In some cases, apparently not. At least they manifest few signs of enthusiasm. Such a " frigid air," however, can gradually be changed if the pastor's heart is aglow.

In a large city the minister and the lay workers find difficulty in gaining access to a vast apartment house. Cliff dwellers do not own their habitations, and they flit from place to place, often in the same city. If they would establish themselves in a church home near by, they might tarry beneath the same roof until the place began to seem like home. In making such contacts the local church can use the mails. If so, the approach through printing ought to be dignified and attractive. As a rule a more personal appeal is preferable. In every apartment building there must be some family that will vouch for the local minister and his lay workers. If the Apostle Paul had served as pastor in an apartment-house district at Ephesus, he would have gained access to those people. He would have asked God to open the door.

Among all the problems we have faced thus far, this one about nomads may seem the most perplexing. At the heart of the solution lies one of the principles that undergird this book: the central importance of the home, and its religion. How can a city become Christian if its families remain pagan? However many and huge the obstacles, the minister and his co-workers should win for Christ and the local church every household for which the Lord God holds them responsible. Was it not while in Ephesus that the apostle wrote: "A great door and effectual is opened unto me, and there are many adversaries" (I Cor.16:9)?

Smaller churches—
less formal.
can compliment new comer
but not usually, esp..
In larger church

XX

The Openings for Evangelism

PASTORAL care and personal work go together. In a sense the one includes the other. The relation between the two ought to be like that between public worship and preaching. To some of us the hour in the sanctuary would seem incomplete without a sermon. On the other hand, if there were nothing but a message from the man of God, our hearts would cry out for praise and prayer. In fact, the whole of pastoral work or of public worship ought to loom up larger than any one part, even though it be the preaching of the Word or the winning of souls.

Why should there be any debate about the relative merits of pastoral care and personal evangelism? Does not the man with the shepherd heart feel much concern about the entire community for which God holds him responsible? Does he not think much concerning the weak and the helpless and every sheep outside the fold? Without going into the distinction between the unsaved and the unchurched, let us consider practical ways and means of finding and winning every person who ought to be serving Christ in the local church. Elsewhere the writer has discussed the matter more fully.[1]

1. *The Quest of the Lost Sheep.* The thesis here ought to seem quite simple. It is that the regular routine of the home-going pastor affords an ideal opportunity to find the stray sheep. Whether unsaved or unchurched, everyone in the community who is not vitally connected with some local church ought to receive the loving care of a shepherd. On the other hand, the home church needs the interest and support of all these persons.

An occasional evangelistic pastor depends largely on special meetings. If the plan works well, who can object? Usually such gatherings appeal only to the faithful members of the flock.

Their souls may be stirred by the evangelist's entreaties for getting right with God. Even in a seminary chapel such a message does more than a little good. The best people in many a sanctuary would " enjoy " sane preaching of this kind more frequently than they have the opportunity. At least numerically, however, the additions to church membership after such meetings do not bulk so large now as in former days.

Meanwhile the minister ought to engage in what one may call pastoral evangelism. By this one means that he strives to present the claims of Jesus Christ to every man, woman, or child who ought to be a member of the home church. Such a pastoral evangelist may or may not hold special services once a year. As for the writer, he commends the practice, especially if the parish minister does the preaching. Even so, the results are likely to come largely through personal work on the part of the pastor and the lay workers. As Henry Ward Beecher used to say, at a time when mass evangelism stood in high favor,[2] the choicest fruit must be hand-picked.

How does the pastoral evangelist start doing personal work? He includes it among his basic plans, beginning with the first days in the new field. In making calls he keeps watching for the lost and the unchurched. From home to home, and in other personal contacts, he strives to learn which of the new friends in the neighborhood is not yet consciously and gladly in vital touch with the Saviour and the local church. Without presuming to know all about the eternal destiny of his new friends, he gradually draws up what has come to be known as " a prospect list." This he keeps largely to himself. " In vain the net is spread in the sight of any bird."

Such a list ought to keep growing. It should also change. Some will unite with the church; others will move out of the parish, or else be carried to the burial ground. In any case, after the first few months of household visitation the prospect list ought to be fairly long. As the minister enters one home after another, he should ascertain which members of the family are not yet enrolled among the communicants. Through the offi-

cers and teachers in the Bible School he can augment the list.
By following pupils to their homes he can find still others who
ought to belong. Unfortunately, a wholesale community can-
vass usually proves inaccurate and disappointing. The com-
piling of a prospect list calls for intensive pastoral work. " You
must go yourself."

Ideally, a man's parish ought to include all the unchurched
and unsaved folk in the community. Such a vision of a man's
field may bring him into a household that should belong to
a neighboring congregation. If so, a sensitive conscience will
keep him from the appearance of evil. Surely it is better to
have overlapping than overlooking. If the Presbyterian minister notifies the Methodist brethren about a new family whom
they have not located, where can there be aught but rejoicing?
Meanwhile every pastor should warn his workers against stealing stray sheep.

In actual experience there need be no gulf between the finding of unchurched people and the resulting appeals on behalf
of Christ. Purely for convenience we are thinking first about
securing the names, and then about winning the friends, one
by one. All the while the minister and his lay helpers ought to
be at work introducing folk to Christ. Such activity may come
to its height during the period leading up to Easter. But why
should there be any " closed season " for the winning of souls?
" Now is the accepted time."

As an ideal for the pastoral evangelist, take a certain minister over in Scotland. In a semirural parish he won the reputation of speaking about the soul to every man or woman, older
boy or girl, in all that countryside. Once in Edinburgh a professor at the divinity school asked a man from the vicinity if the
report were correct. " Yes," said the layman, " I shall never
forget the time years ago when he first spoke to me about my
soul."

Over in Dundee a hundred years ago the mightiest force for
God seems to have been Robert Murray McCheyne.[3] As a
young parish minister, he served there only seven years, for

he died at the age of thirty. Both as a preacher of the Gospel and as a shepherd of souls he won the hearts of countless people. To this very day, all over Scotland, as well as far beyond, his name stands as a symbol of what it means to be a parish minister.

More than half a century later a visiting divine asked an aged saint in Dundee what he remembered most clearly about Robert Murray McCheyne. The layman did not refer to a single pulpit message, or anything public, but told about something personal. As a boy, he had met Pastor McCheyne on the street. Stopping as though the lad were a full-grown man, the dominie inquired about an older sister who had been ill. Then he spoke to the boy about his soul. That was what the fathers used to call " concern." Why not name it " love "?

2. *Bringing the Sheep Into the Fold.* No clergyman now would talk exactly as McCheyne did a hundred years ago. The relations between a pastor and a growing lad today should be less formal. Whatever the verbiage, on the human level the growth of the Kingdom depends largely on " the out-populating power of the Christian stock." In that striking phrase Horace Bushnell set forth the ideal of training and winning all the boys and girls born in homes that belong to the local church. In ways that ought to be well known, the minister strives to enlist for Christ and the congregation every lad or lass within each household. " O satisfy us early with thy mercy; that we may rejoice and be glad all our days " (Ps. 90:14).

Apart from the boys and girls, as well as the youths and maidens, the most fruitful opportunity for parish evangelism may be with young married people. When little children begin to grow up, young parents discover their need of Christ and the Church. In North Jersey year after year a clergyman has had unusual success in gaining recruits. He reports that he and the lay workers find the best " prospects " among the parents of small children. " A little child shall lead them." Meanwhile the church without a soul-winning pastor may find that year after year the members are growing older and fewer.

In still other ways the pastor should do the work of an evangelist. In so far as that calls for enlisting lay workers, the subject belongs under " Parish Administration." [4] Some of the principles appear in the following form letter. It was issued by a young minister who led some of his laymen to do such work. Perhaps because the congregation was only a year old, the stress fell largely on the Church. Unlike many of us who seem, religiously, to be " isolationists," young clergymen to-day are becoming increasingly Church-conscious. Thank God!

" Enlisting recruits for Christ demands individual work with the individual. We hope for a large increase before Easter. The appeal, however, should be made to one person at a time. Men and women enter the Kingdom as they were born into the world, one by one.

" Each visitor should know how to approach the person who ought to be concerned about Christ. During the call be natural. Be friendly. Before many minutes have passed, tell why you have come. When you speak to a man about his spiritual life, you pay him a tribute. Be sure to keep his attention fixed on Christ, not the minister; on the Church, not yourself.

" Form the habit of religious conversation. Without prying, you can ask a man about his religious background. Often there will be some point in common. Thus you can lead his thoughts to the church here in Middletown. The strongest appeal may be personal testimony: ' I have found the church helpful. Come and see.'

" On the other hand, know when not to talk. It is a mistake to apologize. Stress what the home church has accomplished rather than what might have been. Emphasize the present opportunities, not the obstacles. Speak positively, not negatively; suggestively, not exhaustively. Focus the friend's attention; do not scatter his interest.

" High-pressure methods usually defeat themselves. Why argue? Why talk in terms of salesmanship? Money cannot buy what our church has to offer. The love of God is free. Never force anyone to join the church, but encourage everyone who shows interest.

" Let our church stand on its own merits. We are not in competition with any other group. Different ways of worship appeal to various types of people. We are responsible for those who feel at home with our members, and receive help from our ways of worship. If another congregation likewise prospers, thank God.

" At times results appear slowly. What you do now may bear fruit in two or three years. In some cases there may be no visible results.

But the worker never knows when God will turn an unlikely prospect into an ardent disciple. Labor in the spirit of optimism. Since your visit will be remembered, let the recollection be cheerful.

" As the representative of the church, be your very best self. Expect great things from God and attempt great things for Him. Remember that the man whom you find hardest to win may become the most useful member of the church. Pray and work for ' the building up of the church and the gathering to Christ of those whom He loves.' "

After a season of pastoral evangelism, what of the harvest? In any year the visible results may not seem large. Only God can give the increase. Nevertheless, if the minister perseveres aright, the Lord will grant the ingathering. Two of the happiest ministers the writer has met of late reported about the past year's work. The first one had been out of divinity school less than twelve months. The other was a man of middle age. In each case the pastor and his people followed a method like the one outlined above. As a consequence, the work of the Lord revived and the membership of the congregation increased. O for a rising generation of consecrated pastoral evangelists!

Suggested Readings

James, Powhatan W., *George W. Truett: A Biography*. The Macmillan Company, 1939.

Leavell, Roland Q., *Winning Others to Christ*. Baptist Sunday School Board, 1936.

Taylor, Frederick E., *The Evangelistic Church*. The Judson Press, 1927.

Trumbull, Charles G., *Taking Men Alive*. Fleming H. Revell Company, 1938.

XXI

The Treatment of Special Cases

THE diligent pastor meets all kinds of special cases. Once in a while he discovers a friend on the verge of a nervous breakdown. The minister should know enough to urge the calling in of expert medical advice. If the pastor is acquainted with the family physician, it may seem wise to confer with him. As for treatment — other than purely spiritual — that should come from men who have been trained in medical science. At present the discussion concerns less serious degrees of soul disorders, such as every pastor meets again and again.

1. *The Variety of Soul Disorders.* No one but the parish minister, or the family physician, can be aware how much trouble abounds in the hearts of good people today. Lest the following cases seem abnormal, it should be clear that all save one have come under the writer's observation. Not a one involves facts that ought to be kept secret. As for cases that concern the conscience chiefly, we shall postpone them to a later chapter. Each of the friends now in view has been a professing Christian, and almost certainly sincere.

The most common soul malady seems to be fear. Such a feeling of dread calls for sympathy. Who is not tempted to view the unknown future with dire foreboding, and even alarm? In such a case the minister listens until he learns the occasion of the feeling. He may find that it arises from the state of the world today and the sense of helplessness amid forces almost satanic. If so, he can read with the fearful friend Psalm 46, which seems to celebrate the deliverance of Jerusalem when besieged by Sennacherib. The soul treatment here consists in centering the layman's thoughts on God: " God is our refuge and strength."

The stress may fall on the presence of the living Christ. If

so, use Mark 4:35-41. These few words tell how the Master
stilled the storm on the Sea of Galilee. Then he quieted the
hearts of His disciples: " Why are ye so fearful? how is it that
ye have no faith? " Fear must be caused by lack of faith.
Faith must be the God-given remedy for fear. Trust in the
ever-present Christ. He knows. He cares. He is able to deliver
from every dread. Leave with the timorous friend a single
illuminated text. It will serve him again and again as a light
amid soul darkness.

Fear often goes with worry. Fear relates to the future,
whereas worry concerns the present, or the past. Of course
the two terms overlap, just as a sick friend may have typhoid
fever and pneumonia. Once again, the remedy consists in
trusting God and doing His will. The key verse may be Rom.
8:28. Without preaching a little sermon, show how every good
man's steps must be ordered by the Lord. The undergirding
truth ought to be the providence of God.

Feed
so.
faith

inspire

The following excerpt from a letter shows how the believer
overcomes worry. This man of middle age had been struggling
for years with that besetting fault. He had lost his position,
and had been troubled about money. " These past few weeks
have been the most peaceful and satisfactory of my life. I
never could make myself turn loose until a few weeks ago.
Then I asked Jesus to take my life and use it. Since that time
I have had lots of joy and peace, though the contemplation of
wasted years makes me restless and eager to be doing good."
A year later he wrote about the most joyous experiences of his
life. He had learned how to overcome worry by praying to
God and doing His will.

In this case light came chiefly through the fourth chapter
of Philippians. In dealing with believing men and women, one
at a time, the author has used parts of this chapter (ch. 4:1-13,
19) more often than any other portion of the Bible, except a
few psalms. To that friend of middle age the pastor explained
the setting of the chapter: when Paul wrote his " Epistle of
Joy " he was in prison, and penniless. He was awaiting the

Others have financial worries
as well as the preacher

sentence of death, most unjustly. Yet he sent out the happiest of all his letters. In the ensuing conversation about worry, the pastor's emphasis fell on vs. 6 and 7. They show how to escape from worry through prayer, and how to find peace by doing God's will.

Discouragement also enters into such an experience. Such a soul disorder comes often to a man or woman of middle age. The causes may be physical. Even so, the believer in Christ ought to control feelings of gloom and despair. For a time of depression the refrain of Psalms 42 and 43 affords a remedy ready for use. A kindred passage is the nineteenth chapter of First Kings. That dramatic scene in the life of Elijah shows how a strong man of God succumbs to " a fit of the blues " when he begins thinking mainly about himself and his woes. The cure comes through hope in God. This is what Bunyan teaches in his well-known words about " the Slough of Despond."

2. *The Struggle with Doubt.*   Among all the disorders of the soul, none brings more distress than doubt. Especially does it torment the young. Many a youth or maiden needs to learn the truth concerning doubt. It means mental uncertainty about the basic facts of Christianity. Doubt may spring from a man's own wrongdoing, but often there is no such hidden cause. In that case, such a disorder may involve no more moral evil than diphtheria or scarlet fever. Any such disease, however, may lead to anguish and even death. Treat doubt seriously!

These disorders of the soul seem as prevalent among young women of culture as among college men. A prominent woman worker in the Methodist Church, South, once told publicly how as a girl she had struggled with doubt for years. After she had come out on the sunny side, she discovered that her mother and the Bible School teacher, as well as the parish minister, had once gone through such struggles. Why had no one ever explained to her the truth concerning this malady? Every young doubter should have close at hand a spiritual friend and guide.

The experience of young Thomas shows what the honest

doubter needs.[1] After the Resurrection of our Lord, that young man persisted in refusing to believe what he had not seen. When at length he stood face to face with the risen Lord, the malady disappeared from the young man's soul. Those doubts related to the most vital facts of our religion. Whatever a young person may question, or deny, temporarily, the light is almost sure to break when the doubter looks on his problem in the presence of the risen Lord. In dealing with such a case of " honest doubt," the minister can use John 20:28. Anything other than " honest doubt " borders closely on unbelief.[2]

Sometimes a mature woman is troubled lest she be " lost." To everyone but herself this active church worker appears to be a saint. In former years she has been exposed to high-pressure revivalism; now she fears that she has failed to find the pathway to the God she loves. In dealing with such a friend the minister can turn to the sixteenth chapter of The Acts. There he can show her the radically different types of conversion. He points out that a woman like Lydia needs no such soul-crashing experience as that of the stonyhearted Philippian jailer. According to the record in The Acts the soul of the businesswoman responded to good news about Christ much as a flower opens before the rising sun. If the bewildered saint still holds back, the minister can offer her salvation full and free, here and now. In short, she ought to accept the light and then live in joy.

A kindred doubt relates to the Lord's Supper. A man of mature years gives every evidence of being a Christian. Still he refuses to take the Sacrament, lest he sin against grace. He fears that he may eat and drink " damnation." With him the minister should turn to I Cor. 11:29 and explain what the apostle meant by the words better rendered, eat and drink " condemnation." If the pastor knows how to interpret the Scriptures, the light should break and set the shivering friend free from the fog in his soul. Of course the minister should assure himself that the other man's scruples do not arise from unforgiven sins. A case of that sort may call for soul surgery.

This question about the Sacrament also perplexes certain boys and girls, though not so many as formerly. In Henry van Dyke's first pastorate, at Newport, Rhode Island, he found some of his young friends disturbed about those words relating to the Lord's Supper. Hence he formed a class for their instruction. He likewise played with them, and strove to remove their needless scruples. Later in life he protested against the use of fear in bringing a boy or girl into a saving knowledge of Christ. As a lad, Henry himself had been troubled by dread lest he had committed the unpardonable sin. His father, an understanding minister, had told the boy that if any person hated moral evil, this very fact showed the working of the Spirit in his heart.[3]

Some persons old enough to know better grieve over the unpardonable sin. In such a case the minister needs to feel sure that the perturbations do not come from conscious iniquities unconfessed and unforgiven. More often than not, he may find that the victim of these fears holds a distorted idea of the Gospel. Perhaps his former pastors have refrained from preaching doctrine and have left him a prey to irresponsible purveyors of " religious " emotionalism.[4] If so, the minister should give the assurance, on his honor as a Christian gentleman, that there can be no unforgiven sin on the part of any person who has repented and has sought the guidance of the Holy Spirit. Why let a warning against presumption become a barrier to God's grace?

The writer once dealt with a young woman who had given way to such an obsession. Since he was then unmarried, he could not ask his wife to help. In lieu of her aid, he sought out the girl's older sister, and told her what to say. The older sister was more mature than the pastor, and in her tactful way she led the girl into such Christian liberty that life again seemed worth the living. A year afterward the clergyman officiated at the younger sister's marriage to a Christian gentleman. The minister never had ascertained the nature of the young woman's wrongdoing. But he became assured of her repentance and her newness of life in the Saviour.

More difficulty usually attends a minister's dealing with a mature skeptic. In one of his sermons, Dr. Clovis G. Chappell tells of such a man on whom the pastor called at the home.[5] The clergyman found the host disposed to argue, for he was brilliant. At last, almost in despair, the minister led in prayer and then said good night. A little later the skeptic appeared at church, but still as an unbeliever. Afterward, in private conversation, the light began to break when the pastor inquired, " Are you satisfied with life the way you are living it? " The man insisted that he was content, but that night when he knelt to pray with his wife, at last he let his heart have its way. Then the peace of God began to fill his soul. If only one could persuade every such skeptic to attend church and then pray at home, the prospect of many a cure would be bright.

In an army hospital the other day a visiting minister called on a major who had been wounded. Since he did not expect to recover he said to the clergyman: " Padre, I wish I could be sure about the life everlasting. But I cannot believe what I do not understand." In answer to the unspoken question, the clergyman merely said: " Are you sure about your wife? Does she love you? " The major spoke at length about the beauty of his wife's loyalty and devotion, of which the minister had known before he asked the question. Then he said, " Do you understand such love? " Little by little, through this open gateway, the clergyman led the soldier out into the sunlight of " love divine, all loves excelling, joy of heaven, to earth come down." There is always some wise way to deal with an honest doubter.

3. *The Treatment of Soul Disorders.* A study of many such cases would show that scarcely any two of them respond to the same treatment. Nevertheless, a few general facts stand out. One is the need of a minister who knows how to listen. He should do so with every sign of interest and with no ap-

1 if they
try
arguing — little gain

1. Avoid

pearance of being shocked. As George Eliot says more than once in her *Scenes of Clerical Life,* the simple act of confiding in one who cares may bring peace to a troubled soul. The help must come from the Lord, but He has a way of sending it through a pastor who knows Him well and loves Him much. In the prophetic picture of God's Ideal Servant, a good deal of stress falls on hearing: " The Lord God hath opened mine ear, and I was not disobedient " (Isa. 50:5).

Whatever the malady of the troubled soul, the remedy lies at hand in the Scriptures. Of course the Lord can bless the clergyman who relies chiefly on other means of help. Even so, if the lay friend has a religious background, the pastor does well to use a portion of Holy Writ. This way of dealing with a disordered soul appears often in the volume by Dr. John S. Bonnell.[6] As the son of a specialist in mental diseases, this metropolitan divine goes farther in the way of psychiatry than most of his readers should follow. However, his method of relying largely on Scripture seems to be worthy of adoption everywhere.

Frankness leads the writer to acknowledge that in dealing with special cases he has not always met with success. The reference here is not to serious mental collapses, which call for the care of medical specialists. In the treatment of other old-fashioned maladies, such as doubt and fear, or dread of the unpardonable sin, the only man who seems never to fail is the one who almost never tries, or else the one who cannot follow up his " cures." All the while the novice in the art of healing souls ought to face the fact that he may fail almost as frequently as he succeeds. " Not failure, but low aim, is crime."

When one is confronted with an obscure case, what should one do? To shut one's eyes, figuratively, and then guess at the underlying cause, may lead occasionally to an astonishing " cure." Once the writer started a stalled automobile after he had tightened a screw under the front seat! Even so, such methods may show that one is a quack. Would it not be wiser to administer some sort of spiritual placebo, and then ask for a second interview, perhaps a week later? Meanwhile one can pray over the matter, and likewise seek the help of a wise pastoral "consultant." Fortunate is the young clergyman who has formed the habit of seeking aid from a mature physician of the soul. When the two ministers confer about the case in hand, they can usually discover the proper treatment. This the younger man should gladly administer, in the name of the Ideal Physician.

In dealing with a young woman or girl, a pastor of almost the same years may enlist the aid of his wife, or some other gentlewoman not too old. One time a college girl in quest of light came to the home of a young seminary professor. Under non-Christian teachers of psychology and philosophy she had begun to question the fact of God and the reality of her soul. In distress she had gone to the parish minister. Unfortunately, she found him either unwilling or unable to help. Hence he told her: "Forget all about those little things. Dance and play cards and your silly doubts will disappear."

In the home of the teacher the wife did not know how to cope with that modern science, falsely so called. But she could listen and sympathize, as well as read from the Bible and pray. Lovingly, like an older and a younger sister, the two "girls" talked about those "silly doubts" time and again. Little by little, standing on her own feet, the college girl found her way out into the sunlight. From that time onward she almost worshiped the slightly older friend who had taken those troubles to heart and then laid them down at the foot of the Cross.

The spirit of the whole matter breathes out in an old-time hymn that appeals to many a troubled soul today: "Come, ye disconsolate, where'er ye languish." The stress there falls on the plural. In the work of the pastor the appeal should be addressed to one person at a time. At the sanctuary he may preach and pray so as to lift many troubled hearts up into the clear atmosphere where they can behold the living God. In home visitation, however, the minister ought to deal with each anguished spirit alone. Thus the assurance ought to be: "Earth has no sorrows that heaven cannot heal " — right here and right now.

4. The Things to Avoid.   There may be a call for a few negative cautions. One should be obvious: never argue. The debater's method may convince a friend of error, but not persuade him to accept the truth. Again, do not make light of any soul disorder. However fanciful or nonsensical the obsession seems to the ministerial observer, a molehill can look as big as a mountain when a friend is down in the dumps. For much the same reason, never indulge in satire. At home and in the office of the family physician the troubled friend may have endured all sorts of sarcasm. At last, like Job, the tortured soul may cry out: " Miserable comforters are ye all "! Why should a minister of Christ imitate one of Job's tormentors? They talked too much, and were unkind. They did not even try to be just. Why did they not keep quiet?

Once more, do not despair. The Lord has a way of bringing heart's ease through the " healing presence " of a minister who may not know how to treat the trouble in hand. The late Professor George Herbert Palmer used to tell about some problem that arose in his life as a college student. Having made an evening appointment with Phillips Brooks, the young man went to talk things over. On the way home that night young Palmer felt at peace with God and men. All at once he remembered that he had not mentioned his trouble to Phillips Brooks. In that genial presence the student's distress of heart had melted away like Boston snow in the warmth of the April sun.

Even Phillips Brooks might not have been able to help inquirers during the ten years of his ministry at Philadelphia. Only after the clergyman moved to Boston does he appear to have become expert in dealing with all kinds of spiritual trouble. The same principle holds true among doctors. According to a revered professor at the Harvard Medical School, " one cannot expect to become a skilled practitioner of medicine in the four or five years allotted to the medical course." How much more does that prove to be the case after a young man

Time + grace heal all things — 90% time 10% grace

— Dr. R.T. Williams Nazarine Chure

has spent twenty-four months in theoretical study at the divinity school!

However, let no minister despair. In due time he can excel as a physician of the soul. Let him keep on dealing with cases, one after another, as they arise in his routine work. Growing experience will result in larger skill, as well as the kind of self-confidence that never becomes presumption. More and more will the pastor's spirit of trust in God prove contagious, or rather, infectious. As he lives close to the Lord, and learns how to love people, he will unconsciously acquire a " healing presence." Reverently, one after another of his parish friends will say about this servant of God, " He restoreth my soul."

Suggested Readings

Dollard, John, *Victory Over Fear.* Reynal & Hitchcock, Inc., 1942.

Elliott, H. S., and G. L., *Solving Personal Problems.* Henry Holt and Company, Inc., 1936.

Holman, Charles T., *The Cure of Souls.* The University of Chicago Press, 1932.

Oliver, John R., *Psychiatry and Mental Health.* Charles Scribner's Sons, 1932.

1. let the men talk —
2. In your own strength you can do nothing
3. some moral problem Behind most complaining
4. never betray a confidence
5. dont stir up more trouble than can handle — as family — strive for truth

XXII

The Handling of Moral Problems

A SERIOUS moral problem in the parish may test every fiber of the pastor's soul. Not to deal with the issue would mean to shirk the path of duty. To handle the case adequately requires the expenditure of nervous energy, as well as hours of time. If he fails he may have to face serious consequences. Nevertheless, the man called of God does not flinch. Almost every minister worth his salt has dealt with cases such as appear below. Each of them comes out of real life.

If such experiences do not befall any young pastor, why should he despair? Let him not go out in quest of moral issues. Sooner or later he will find one lying on his doorstep. After that will arise another problem of a different kind, equally baffling. Each of them will have to be handled in a different fashion. There can be no patent way of dealing with a person in moral distress. As in the medical world the physician rarely finds " a textbook case," so in the minister's parish work things seldom run true to classroom theories. Even so, it should help the pastor to consider a number of concrete cases.

1. *The Settling of Bitter Disputes.* Ofttimes the minister ought to serve as a peacemaker. In a rural parish two active lay officers would not speak to each other. They had quarreled about a line fence. If they had not been blessed with self-restraint, they might have come to blows. As soon as the pastor learned of the trouble, through proper channels, he called on one farmer and then on the other. In vain the minister pleaded for a reconciliation. Then he arranged for a meeting with the two at his study in the church. Before he entered into any discussion he read a few of our Lord's words about a man's being reconciled to his brother.

Then the minister prayed briefly for his two friends, naming the older one first. After leading in the Lord's Prayer, which resembled a solo, he asked them to pray, without suggesting which one should lead. First the older man spoke to the Lord, haltingly, and the other layman followed, falteringly. When the three friends arose from their knees, the two laymen shook hands. The pastor left them at once, after a word of thanks. The next day the two farmers worked together in rebuilding that line fence. Thereafter they loved each other more than ever. They also thought highly of their pastor: " A brave man, and a true friend! "

Sometimes the dispute involves the women of two households, more than the men. If so, the pastor needs insight and courage, as well as tact and perseverance. In a parish not far from us a lay officer called at the parsonage to report that he and his wife felt obliged to leave the church. They liked the minister and his wife, as well as the people, except two other married folk. They too were active in the work of the congregation. The relations among the four had become so strained that it seemed wise for the first couple to withdraw from the scene of strife.

The minister thanked his friend for coming and then asked him to do nothing for a week. As yet the pastor did not see a glimmering of light. First of all, he prayed for guidance. That evening he called on the other two friends, at a time when both were at home. He found them openly belligerent, especially the wife. In so far as the " peacemaker " could judge, there had been wrong, or at least indiscretion, on both sides. The dispute had originated between the two women, and each husband had vowed to stand by his spouse. For the first time in all his days, the pastor felt that he was about to witness the meeting of an irresistible force with an unmovable object.

Being a man of courage and action, the minister invited all four erstwhile friends to meet him at the study the next evening. There he greeted them warmly. Without any explanation or apology he read the thirteenth chapter of First Corinthians. After a short prayer for the home church, and for his four friends there present, he asked them to talk the matter over together. Then he sat in silence. With heart half broken he learned how far good people can go when they yield to a divisive spirit. On and on the verbal conflict raged, with much more heat than light.

At last the minister felt that all their venom had been poured forth. Then he spoke out, asking the friends to forgive each other, then and there. He based the plea on their love for Christ and the Church. He had figured out that the men were anxious for a reconciliation, and that the women were waiting for some pretext to abandon their battle lines. Even so, the pastor insisted that their reconciliation should be on a Christian basis. Ere they could be friends, in the right meaning of that term, they must make confession, both to God and to each other. That they seemed willing to do.

Before the five of them parted that night, they all knelt down to pray. The minister led in the confession of sins. Then he voiced the assurance of God's pardon for every wrong confessed, provided it were made right, in so far as doing so lay in human hands. He closed the prayer with fervent entreaties for " the peace and prosperity " of the home church. After he had pronounced the benediction they all arose. The women embraced each other and the two laymen shook hands. The minister found it hard to keep back his tears. On that one case he had worked harder than on any assignment in all his school days, and perhaps he had learned more. What a laboratory is life!

Another minister located in a new field a few weeks before the annual congregational meeting. There he had to referee what might have resulted in a free-for-all verbal fight. Somehow the Scotch-Irish excel in that kind of conflict. In this case more than a few of the leading people protested against the election of two men from the same household, who would sit together on the official board. Either one would have been acceptable. The objectors stated their position strongly. In the balloting they won by a majority. Not long afterward the minister learned that the offended family intended to leave the church of their fathers. If they had done so, there might have been a vertical split in the church body, with two factions almost equal in strength and vigor.

To this one case the pastor gave most of his waking hours for more than a week. First he went to the leading members of the aggressive party, one after another. With them he made little progress. He found them kind to him personally, but not disposed to feel any sense of regret. Perhaps he agreed with them that in a large congregation there should be a more equitable method of nominating members for the official board. If so, he did not broach that subject during the existing crisis. Rather did he plead for the welfare of the home church, that there might be peace. With the leaders on the other side also he made no headway.

At length he saw that he was getting nowhere by going from man to man. Then the minister decided to follow the Biblical injunction. The Master says that when every personal appeal has failed, a man is to take with him the elders of the church. In company with two or three representative laymen, who had not entered hitherto into the discussion, the pastor called on one leader after another. At length all concerned agreed to forgive and be friends, for the sake of their beloved church. A little later the minister doubtless led the official board in devising a more equitable method of nominating leaders of the flock. Fortunately, he had averted a split in the church. The way to deal with such a problem is through pastoral work, in the spirit of prayer.

2. *The Wrong Use of Money.* Difficult problems often relate to the misuse of money. The following case appears in an excellent book from England.[1] The author tells about a girl eighteen years of age who came to her pastor and confessed the sin of theft. In the drapery store where she was employed at starvation wages she had stolen sums amounting to fifty pounds. The excuse was her small earnings and her love of finery. She knew that her wrongdoing was about to be dis-

closed. In terror she fled to her pastor. Her penitence seemed
to him sincere, for she exclaimed, again and again: " I have
been a wicked girl! What can I do? "

The minister urged that she tell her parents, at least her
mother. The girl refused, absolutely. Neither would she go
to her employer. She loved her parents and she feared her
" boss." At length the pastor reluctantly agreed to lend her
the fifty pounds. Not being a man of means, he had to borrow
the money, which she was to repay in weekly installments. So
she did, for a while. She also attended church and Bible school.
Then she began to slip back, surreptitiously, into her old ways.
She was apprehended for these latter thefts. While the law was
taking its course she told her pastor: " You seemed to get the
money so easily! " He in turn felt that he had played the fool.

The British author declares that such an experience throws
light on the Atonement: " Easy forgiveness involves imper-
fect repentance. Result — no assurance of God's forgiveness,
no permanent reformation." What should that money-lending
minister have done? He might have taken the girl to her parents, at least one of them. If she refused to go, he could have
summoned them to his study. In their presence he might have
told her to confess. Then he might have left the girl alone with
her mother and father, or one of them. Thus far there could
have been some other procedure.

About one fact there can be no question. The pastor should
not have become personally responsible for the payment of
any financial obligation. On the other hand, with the girl's
consent, he might have gone to the employer and pleaded for
mercy. All the while the pastor should have striven to bring
the culprit into right relations with her God. This the minister tried to do, but not wisely. He made the wages of sin seem
too little. He failed to teach Christian ethics, as well as Biblical
doctrine. As Dr. Gillie suggests, these cases throw light on the
proper response to the Atonement.

One of our most helpful writers about the Cross [2] would
agree with Dr. Gillie. The current author recounts the experi-

ence of the late C. F. Andrews. That clergyman had to deal with
a man of birth and culture, who was living as a wastrel in the
slums of East London. This derelict had even stolen some of
the silver vessels used in the parish church for administering
Communion to the sick. Late one night he appeared on the
doorstep of the clergyman's abode. In " an utterly befuddled
state " the man " produced the vessels from his ragged pocket."

" Andrews' first impulse had been to take him in again but,
having sought for guidance, he decided to do a thing he had
never done before — to give the man into custody. Next morning he appeared with the man in court and asked that a light
sentence might be given. As a result the man was sent to prison
for a month on condition that Andrews would care for him
when he was released. So Andrews stood alongside him in his
punishment and in his rehabilitation. When, much later, he
was asked whether he thought Andrews had done the right
thing . . . , he answered, ' Yes, sir; that was the turning-
point of my life; for if you had taken me into the mission
house I should have gone straight back to the drink the very
next morning.' "

Professor Dillistone observes that here we have " a submis-
sion to justice, coupled with a deep identification with the
guilty one; here, surely, is a reproduction . . . of the Cross."
Would that every student of theology might sit under such an
interpreter of the Atonement! Much the same message comes
from former Dean Charles R. Brown.[3] One night he was
preaching on God's " Mercy." At the end of the service a
young man came to the study and confessed his sin. As the
cashier of a manufacturing concern he had stolen $2,800.
Knowing that the day of reckoning was drawing near, he con-
templated suicide or flight.

The two men talked until midnight. Together they devised
and carried out a practical plan. It led to the confession of the
defalcation, and the retention of the young man at his work
while he was repaying the entire amount. That called for several years of self-sacrifice. Meanwhile the pastor had witnessed

the recovery of " honest manhood." Here follows the com-
ment of Dean Brown: " What if I had been trifling with some
fringe of truth that night? . . . You can always count upon
the presence of a thief or two in almost any evening congregation." One is tempted to ask: What if there had been no hour
of public worship in town that evening? What if the minister
later that night had not known how to deal with a penitent
thief in the spirit of the Cross?

> " The dying thief rejoiced to see
> That fountain in his day;
> And there may I, as vile as he,
> Wash all my sins away."

3. *The Problem of Drunkenness.* Some of a minister's
worst defeats come in dealing with men and women who drink
to excess. The writer has had a larger proportion of failures
with such cases than with any other maladies of the soul. He
has found that the man who drinks hard may when sober be
abounding in charm. For the woman who stoops to such sin,
the author has long felt a world of sympathy. In view of his
own failures, it is a pleasure to record the successes of a Baptist minister.[4] He reports experiences with two drunken men,
each of whom became a Christian and a total abstainer.

In each case the cure was brought about, on the human level,
by kindness and tact. With one man while intoxicated in a
barber shop the minister took the part of the Good Samaritan.
With the other he made effective use of a hobby, which was
working with wood. Since the man in view labored as a carpenter, when not deep in his cups, the pastor sought him out at
the shop. There the talk began about wood and tools. Erelong
the two were conversing about the Carpenter of Nazareth.
Through Him and His Cross the victim of drink found the
way to become a consistent Christian, as well as a noble husband and father. In each case above, the entering wedge seems
to have been the pastor's refusal to humiliate a brother man
when under the influence of liquor.

If strong drink enslaves a woman of culture, the case may seem almost hopeless. She may be striving in vain to escape from intolerable conditions at home. Her brilliant husband may be a brute when inflamed from his cups. Such a case appears in the tale by George Eliot, " Janet's Repentance." A study of this narrative should help to prepare any minister for dealing gently with such a friend. In George Eliot's tale the clergyman seems not to have been a genius, but surely he was a saint. By the sort of methods we have considered already, he gradually led Janet Dempster into the sunlight of Christian victory. These are excerpts from the novel:

" Janet felt she was alone. No human soul had measured her anguish. . . . If there was any divine pity, she could not feel it. . . . She wanted strength to do right. She wanted something to rely on besides her own resolutions. [She needed a Christlike pastor.] The impulse to confession requires the presence of a fresh ear and a fresh heart. In our moments of spiritual need, the man to whom we have no tie but our common nature seems nearer than mother, brother, or friend. . . . The tale of divine pity was never yet believed from lips that were not moved by human pity. . . .

" The great source of courage, the great help to perseverance, was the sense that she had a friend and teacher in Mr. Tryan. She could confess her difficulties to him. She knew that he prayed for her. . . . The act of confiding in human sympathy . . . prepared her soul for that stronger leap by which faith grasps the idea of the divine sympathy." [5]

For encouragement of a different kind turn to a present-day movement, " Alcoholics Anonymous." These unknown friends do not claim to cure every case with which they deal, but neither do the psychiatrists. The volunteer workers in Alcoholics Anonymous have themselves been set free from such slavery. They estimate that they succeed at the time with 50 per cent of their cases, and that they win out later with another 25 per cent. Thus they confess failure in one case out of four. A high percentage of cures! Strange to tell, they re-

port their chief successes among the worst cases. Without being sectarian, this movement seems to be distinctly religious.
It calls on the victim of drink to stand out-and-out for God.

The spirit of the appeal sounds forth in the following slo-
gan: " Give God the first ten minutes of every day and He will
give you the whole twenty-four hours back all different."
From this point of view one of the former drunkards has written: " When we sincerely took such a position all sorts of things
followed. On such a footing we became less and less interested
in ourselves. More and more we became interested in what we
could contribute to life. As we felt new power flow in, as we
enjoyed new peace of mind, as we discovered we could face
life successfully, we began to lose our fear of today, tomorrow, or the hereafter. We were reborn." [6]

Sometimes the minister's problem concerns illegal selling of
liquor. During the days of Prohibition a Negro pastor on
Edisto Island, South Carolina, learned that one of his lay officers was selling " bootleg whisky." The minister called on the
culprit and expostulated with him kindly, but to no avail. The
layman felt aggrieved. He said that he gave a good deal of his
money to the church, and that his wife played the organ. He
also declared that unless the pastor dropped the matter at once
and forever, the affluent pair would leave the church and join
another. The minister called a meeting of his official board and
explained the facts. Then they went in a body to call on the
recalcitrant brother, who had not attended the meeting, though
he had been specially invited.

Despite all that the clergyman and his lay brethren could
do, the offended official and his spouse left the church and
joined another in the neighborhood. Of course they could not
take letters of honorable dismissal. These facts became known
to the writer through his friends on the island. Those white
folk praised the minister for his high sense of loyalty and for
his courage. Now the question arises: Did the Negro brother
succeed or did he fail? If he acted tactfully, as he seems to have
done, he surely must have received the blessing of God. Now

that liquor flows freely among us everywhere, such problems will surely increase. Will every white pastor be as brave?

4. *The Case of Suicide.* Occasionally a minister has to deal with a case of attempted suicide. It is wise to think about the matter beforehand, as there may be a call for instant action. Unfortunately, this cowardly practice seems to be growing more common. A recent novel describes the sense of frustration that may lead to self-murder. An elderly man is telling his devoted daughter why he is about to " end it all." Meanwhile one feels that a kind and loving pastor could have helped avert that tragedy. Here is part of the short cruel note:

" There was another woman who tried to make the best of me, — your mother. . . . What I am going to do will hurt you, but not so much as she was hurt. After all, old girl, it's no good sitting in an empty theater after the play is over and the curtain's rung down. The thing to do is to get up and go; and that is what I am about to do. I love you very much; I only wish I'd realized how much long, long ago." Without casting any stones at such a hopeless mortal, one feels that a sympathetic pastor could have pointed out a better path of escape from such frustration.

On an earlier page of this novel a physician is speaking about a case of suicide: " He was fed up. He had been on the dole for three years and was sick to death of everything. . . . In desperation he'd come to me and I'd offered him platitudes and coloured water. You know, that night I learned a lesson. All that man needed was someone to listen to his troubles and sympathize and advise; to make him feel that he wasn't finished and done; to give him confidence to go out and take the world by the throat, instead of cutting his own." In sooth, the man needed to " try God." [7]

Once the writer had an experience with a man of middle age who had committed murder. A few years after he had begun to serve a life sentence in the penitentiary, he asked for admission to our church, *in absentia.* Since his penitence seemed sincere and humble, he was accepted as a regular communicant.

Whenever the people of the Lord assembled to celebrate the Sacrament, that same afternoon the minister and one of the lay officers would go to the penitentiary and administer the Communion to another of God's children, who dwelt there in a little upper room.

This case led the minister to commit a blunder of a sort that is common among " men of the cloth." Back in the home town friends of the prisoner drew up a petition asking the governor to release him on parole. This paper the minister signed; he also wrote a letter endorsing the plea. After full investigation the chief executive denied the request, and told the pastor why. If the dominie had known the facts, he would never have taken part in that ill-advised movement. Fortunately for his later peace of mind, he wrote the governor a letter of apology, and the two remained friends. Once again the parson learned not to think of himself more highly than he ought to think.

5. *The Attitude of the Minister.* Whatever the nature and the enormity of the transgression in view, the attitude of the clergyman counts for more than anything he can say or do. Does he really care? Can he listen? Before he speaks or acts, does he learn all he ought to know? On the other hand, does he refrain from needless probing of the shivering soul? Does he put himself in the other person's place, and then look on the moral guilt with mercy? This is what one means by viewing every such problem as it looms forth in the light of the Cross.

Here comes wise counsel from that minister over in England: " In all such cases there are two rules. First, there is always a right course of action. At all costs it is to be found and followed. There can be no peace or progress through moral compromise. A sin cannot be left behind unless there is real repentance, and repentance means reversal of attitude. . . . Secondly, strive to make the inquirer discover for himself what is right. Never assert your own authority, but the authority of God. There are many of these difficult subjects on which the Lord has left us clear guidance. His words ought to be final with us all. Try to bring the sinner into living contact with the divine instructions. You cannot wholly fail if you succeed in doing that." [8]

There is need, also, of practical wisdom. That will keep a man from taking sides in any dispute. He should never advise an outraged wife to apply for a divorce. If later she decides that she has made a mistake, she should have no excuse for blaming her pastor. The same principle holds true in a church quarrel. The man of God should serve as the friend and guide of the whole congregation. If he proves not large-minded enough to shepherd the whole flock, his littleness may lead to a divided church.

Fortunately, no minister needs to face these problems alone. Not only can he look to God for help; ofttimes he can discover the will of the Lord by consulting a neighboring pastor. In no other way can a novice handle such cases skillfully. Thus without cost he can have a sort of " internship " under a master of his own choosing. As for the older man who has the heart of a shepherd, he will thank God for a younger minister who never loses sight of a single sheep.

Among the lay officers, likewise, or else the godly women, there may be a discerning soul whose counsel will prove better than gold. Here again, all that is said about the case ought to be in confidence. The pastor has no right to divulge what he learns as a representative of the Lord. Without mentioning any names, however, he can explain the situation and receive the needed help. Under God, there is always something for the pastor to say or do when he comes face to face with a problem of conscience.

In preparing his heart for ministering to a friend with a moral problem, the minister should read The Epistle to the Hebrews, especially the latter portion of the second chapter, and the fourth. Have we not in Christ Jesus a merciful and faithful High Priest? " Let us therefore come boldly unto the throne of grace, that we may obtain mercy, and find grace to help in time of need " (Heb. 4:16).

Suggested Readings

Hadfield, J. A., *Psychology and Morals*. Robert M. McBride & Company, 1925.
Holman, Charles T., *Getting Down to Cases*. The Macmillan Company, 1942.
Stolz, Karl R., *The Church and Psychotherapy*. Abingdon-Cokesbury Press, 1943.

XXIII

The Attitude Toward Sex Tangles

THE most bewildering of moral problems may be those relating to sex. The present writer deplores the current emphasis on the subject. With many others he feels that such discussions often do more harm than good. They tend to inflame what they strive to allay. Nevertheless, the pastor must work in a world abnormally aware of sex in its slimiest depths. As a physician of the soul he should be ready to deal with such cases as they arise. The number and the variety will depend on the size and the character of the community. Much more will depend on the minister's reputation as a personal counselor, and on his ability to help everyone who applies for aid in solving one of these nasty problems. Such a reputation quickly spreads throughout the parish. So does the fact that a minister seems helpless when he confronts a case involving sex.

Especially does the chaplain need such ability. To his amazement many a chaplain has discovered that his chief opportunity comes in personal counseling, and that the majority of the problems have something to do with sex. Ofttimes he finds that the root of the matter lies back in the boy's home. In fact, the padre may feel tempted to think Freud right in presenting sex as the major factor in human life. Gradually, however, the padre should get his bearings. Through manifold experiences as a friend and brother of the soldier or sailor in distress because of sex, the chaplain should be making ready to become the ideal pastor of tomorrow. What, then, will he meet in his parish work?

1. *The Problem of Divorce.* Because of the war, divorces are sure to abound. In truth, they have been with us through the years, more and more. Here we are concerned, not with the numbers and the causes, but with the treatment by the pastor. Hence we turn to cases from life.

A woman forty years of age called on a neighboring minister, whom she knew by sight and reputation. Without going far into the facts she asked if she ought to secure a divorce. According to her account, which seemed to be correct, she had abundant reason, on the ground of her husband's adultery, willful and repeated. Instead of probing into secrets that she rightly felt loath to reveal, the clergyman inquired about her two children, aged ten and twelve. He found that the boy and the girl dearly loved their father, as well as their mother. If the news of an impending divorce became public, their hearts would be broken. She would not know how to make the matter clear to the children.

In such a case the minister of the Gospel should never make the decision. Neither should he try to force his opinion on the other person. This time the clergyman thanked the woman for coming, and inquired if there were anything else on her heart. Then he offered prayer for the family, including by name the father and the mother, as well as each child. Rising from the chair at which he had bowed down, he shook hands with his new friend. Then he said three things, in substance: " Come to me again whenever you wish to talk things over. Pray for guidance from above. Unless you are sure about the path of duty, do nothing. Wait on the Lord. ' In all thy ways acknowledge him, and he shall direct thy paths ' " (Prov. 3:6).

This text he left shining in her soul. The verse comes out of the one Bible book that deals most frankly and fully with problems relating to sex. How could a pastor do his work if he did not know the book of The Proverbs? In this case the minister kept on praying. He also asked the most winsome of his church visitors, all of them mature women, to call on his new friend, somewhat casually, and get her interested in the local church. Of course he did not tell any of them why he made the request. Six months after the first interview he again welcomed his friend at the study. This time he saw that she had been transformed. She had learned how to pour out her heart before the Lord.

The wife came to thank her " pastor " for his wise counsel. She did not tell him much about what had occurred between husband and wife. Perhaps she had been partly at fault, though not through improper relations with any man. She made clear, however, that God had answered unceasing prayer. Her husband had confessed his wrongdoing, and had tried to make what few amends lay within his power. He had determined that as long as they both lived he would love her and cherish her, according to the ordinance of God. In later years that husband and father fulfilled his covenant vows. Never again did he bring such anguish to that wife.

In another case a different pastor learned from the husband that he was applying for a divorce. Here also the minister pleaded for inaction, but this time to no avail. The same afternoon in a conference with the wife he saw no reason for hope. Each of the parties suspected the other of marital infidelity. The two had likewise quarreled about the distribution of money. Unfortunately, they had no children. As in most other cases of divorce, these three factors bulked large: disputes arising out of intimate sexual relations, out of there being no children, and out of failure to agree about money. If there were no obsession about sex, no love for little children, and no concern about money, there might be few divorces. But there might also be few marriages!

In the case before us the pastor seemed to have failed. Instead of regretting the time he had " wasted," he kept on spending still more time. Every little while he would call on the former husband, an attorney, at the office, but not during the busiest hours. The minister also went to see the former wife at her home. With neither of them had the clergyman taken sides. He felt that, as in most cases of the sort, both parties had been at fault, chiefly in not understanding each other. Hence he strove to bring each of them into closer relations with God.

One day the former husband told his pastor and friend: " I feel that our divorce was a mistake. I find that I love my

former wife. I know now that she never was untrue to me."
The minister thanked him for this confidence, and then asked
his friend's permission to tell the former wife. That was
granted, gladly. Making an appointment by telephone, the
pastor went at once to her home. There the good news met
with a joyous reception. With tears in her eyes the woman
said: " After these six months of separation I love him more
than ever. I know now that he never was unfaithful. I wish
the courts had kept us apart for six months, by putting us on
probation. Then we could have lived together again."

Once in his life that clergyman gladly officiated at the remarriage of two persons each of whom had been divorced recently,
and not on " Scriptural grounds." In his pulpit work thereafter the minister kept explaining at times what the Lord
Jesus taught about marriage and divorce. However, he had
learned to refrain from harsh denunciations. If there were
more of loving Christian nurture on the part of ministers,
there might be fewer divorces among Church members.

In another congregation a young woman served as the organist. She had secured a divorce five years before a young
minister entered the field. Later she had fallen in love with a
Christian gentleman who had proposed marriage. The two of
them came to their new friend, a recent graduate from the
seminary, and asked him to perform the ceremony. They
wished to be married publicly in the sanctuary, as both the
families belonged to the church, and each household had a
host of friends.

The young clergyman did not know what to do or say.
Hesitantly he replied that he would ask the official board if
they would grant the use of the church for that purpose. Ordinarily such a request comes from the bride's parents, but this
time the minister had to do something, and do it soon. Since
he did not know what action to desire from the official board,
he postponed the issue until he could see the light. In his branch
of the Church Ecumenical divorce is allowed, though it is not
mandatory, on the " Scriptural grounds " of adultery, or will-

ful and permanent desertion. As a rule such a desertion seems equivalent to adultery.

After he had prayed alone, the bewildered young parson went to a mature pastor who was known as a man of wisdom and honor. This older minister listened to a recital of the facts. Then he advised the young man to request the permission of his official board, not only for the use of the church, but for the pastor to officiate at the ceremony. Of course these two factors went together. What concerned the two ministers of Christ was the ethical problem of the pastor. The older man's way of reasoning ought to help other clergymen in dealing with like situations:

" The principle underlying the whole matter concerns the duration of marriage. According to the Scriptures, it ought to last as long as both the parties live. If either of them dies, the marriage bonds are dissolved, then and there. Decency should forbid the survivor to think about remarriage soon after the funeral, but the laws of God do not specify any set period of waiting. If either party to a marriage commits adultery, especially when it is deliberate and oft-repeated, that marriage may be said to be dead.

" The same principle holds true of willful and permanent desertion. In either case the innocent party, who has secured the divorce on Scriptural grounds, should be free to remarry if he or she feels so led of God. In applying these principles, be careful. Have nothing to do with the remarriage of divorced persons, neither of whom belongs to your church. When you feel a personal responsibility about a member of your flock, wait until you are sure before you agree to officiate. Never pronounce the blessing of God on a remarriage unless you feel certain about His sanction. If in doubt, don't! "

2. *The Treatment of Unmarried Offenders.* Another pastor sought counsel regarding a young girl who had " loved not wisely but too well." Especially since the girl was subnormal mentally, the mother had feared to tell the father, lest he shoot the young fellow who had wronged her. The mother had gone

to the minister for advice. Not knowing what to say, he had counseled her to do nothing until the light broke. Then they two prayed for that light. The case was complicated by the fact that the male culprit's parents were prominent in the same church. Up to that time the young seminary graduate had never faced such a problem. What did he learn from his older friend?

The mature clergyman waited until he had heard the facts. Then he inquired about the physician in the girl's family. Learning that the doctor concerned was a leading layman in the church, and a noble Christian gentleman, the older minister advised his young friend to put the case before the physician and do exactly as he proposed. Fortunately, the doctor offered to take the matter into his own hands. First he went to the father of the girl and told him the situation, of which the physician had not heard previously. After an explosion of temper on the part of the father, the two men worked together in doing what little they could to make the best out of a sordid mess. Thus the young minister found that there could be no quick and easy way of dealing with many a case involving sex. He had to call in the help of two experts, one a clergyman and the other a physician.

Such cases often end disastrously. A woman of middle age sobbed as she told her pastor about indignities that had been heaped on her eighteen-year-old son. She insisted that he was " a perfect darling, as innocent as a babe." He had been arrested for the alleged rape of a girl below the legal age of consent. Once again, the minister was inexperienced. Knowing the woman to be truthful, he accepted her version of the facts. By personal interviews and in various other ways he strove to prevent the matter from going into court. He met with such rebuffs that he felt the city officials must be heartless.

At length the case came to trial. The pastor went to the courtroom, where he sat with the lad's parents. Within an hour he heard the verdict, " Guilty! " After he had listened to the evidence, which proved revolting, he knew that the verdict must be just. So did the parents, to their amazement and horror. The minister likewise saw why his pleas for mercy had met with a stony response. With the city officials he saw that the law had to take its course. Meanwhile he strove to comfort the parents and help the lad who had done the wrong.

One thing the pastor failed to do. He should have written each of the city officials a letter of regret for the attempt to interfere with justice. He might also have written the wise men who report cases of the sort and inquired why the authors almost never record their failures. Those experts seem seldom to make a mistake in diagnosis, or to fail in working a complete cure. Surely it can never be so with the average pastor. He lives among his people. In time he discovers that he is neither inspired nor infallible. His failures tend to keep him humble. They likewise make him cautious. In the case before us, the pastor should first have gone to the city officials for their version of the facts, and not to plead for mistaken " mercy."

A zealous minister can be too avid in his desire to learn all the facts. Recently a young man went to a city pastor and confessed the sin of adultery. He wished to ascertain what he should do to find peace of heart. Instead of listening, in the spirit of prayer, the clergyman started to probe the wound. He wanted to know when and where the deeds had been done, and other details of a sort likely to gratify morbid curiosity. Soon the penitent youth became disgusted and left the study. To this day the parson feels hurt. Why did the young fellow terminate the interview so suddenly? At least he might have remained long enough to tell the " preacher " what he wished to know about the ways of the underworld. Why too did the fellow never return? Such queries suggest their own answers. But who can tell what became of that young penitent after such ministerial mishandling?

Another experience concerned a young woman. She came to a local minister old enough to be her father. Almost as soon as she had begun to tell about her sins of impurity, he stopped her: " Let me send for my wife. She and I always work out such problems together." It happened that the young woman knew about the wife. The guilty girl wanted to talk things over with an ordained minister of Jesus Christ. When she found that she had gone to the wrong one, she left at once. Then the pastor submitted the case to a professor who dealt with such matters. The decision was that the incident had been closed. When a patient knowingly suffers once from malpractice, she seeks another surgeon.

Sometimes the problem concerns the ethics of confession. A man of middle age sought out his pastor and confessed the sin of adultery. Knowing the layman well, the minister felt certain that the repentance was sincere and deep-seated. He also assured himself that the matter was closed. Humanly speaking, there would be no repercussions. Still the transgressor wanted to find peace. Should he appear before the consistory — the governing board — and confess his sin? Above all, ought he to tell his wife?

Thus far the pastor had listened. When the lay friend became silent, the minister assured him of pardon, cleansing, and peace, on the basis of sincere confession and a resolute desire to make all possible amends. More than once the pastor quoted I John 1:9, as well as v. 7. As for confession, he explained that it ought to be as wide as the offense, and no wider. Also he made clear that confession before men should be limited to persons with whom it would do good.

Further the minister declined to go. In his heart he felt that no good could come from telling the church officials or the wife. But both these problems rested with the man who had done the wrong. After the two friends had prayed together, the layman said that his problem had been solved. There would be no further confessions. The pastor expressed his approval of that course. Later he was responsible, indirectly, for the layman's becoming a trustee of the local church. Thus the transgressor became assured of pardon, both from God and from men.

Why multiply cases, whether or not the treatment results

in a cure? We have gone far enough to conclude that the minister who deals with the malady known as sex must seek a wisdom higher than his own. " If any of you lack wisdom, let him ask of God, that giveth to all men liberally, and upbraideth not; and it shall be given him. But let him ask in faith, nothing wavering " (James 1:5, 6).

Suggested Readings

Cabot, Richard C., M.D., *Christianity and Sex*. The Macmillan Company, 1937.

Dexter, E., and R., *The Minister and Family Problems*. Richard R. Smith, 1931.

Gray, A. Herbert, *Men, Women, and God*. Association Press, 1938.

Groves, Ernest R., *Conserving Marriage and the Family*. The Macmillan Company, 1944.

Piper, Otto A., *The Christian Interpretation of Sex*. Charles Scribner's Sons, 1941.

Weatherhead, Leslie D., and Greaves, Marion, *The Mastery of Sex Through Psychology and Religion*. Student Christian Movement Press, London, 1931.

XXIV

The Value of a "Pastor's Hour"

SOONER or later every pastor ought to face the question: " Will the people come to me with their problems? " In a rural parish that may not prove feasible. The friends may seem unwilling to alter their customs. They may not wish to put the minister on the same level as the doctor. In many an urban congregation, however, there should be an opening for this kind of pastoral work. What does it matter where the minister deals with people, if he employs divine truth in meeting human needs?

1. *The Meaning of the Title.* The writer prefers to speak of " The Pastor's Hour." Others say " The Protestant Confessional," or " The Pastor's Clinic." The word confessional might suggest an infusion of Roman Catholicism. A clinic would call for a staff of specialists, such as only a wealthy metropolitan church could afford. On the other hand, any mature parish minister can set apart certain weekday hours when he will be alone in the study, and ready to meet the friend who wishes to talk about things spiritual. For the practical workings of such a plan read *The Green Light,* by the well-known novelist Lloyd C. Douglas.

The pastor's hour calls for a quiet place of meeting. If possible, it should be in the church, with hallowed associations. The minister's home might suggest the sharing of secrets with other members of the household. While the pastor alone remains in the room with the person who calls, someone else ought to be within easy reach. Ordinarily the clergyman sits on one side of a flat table and the visitor on the other side, not too close. The fact that in this room others have found courage and strength, as well as peace and joy, ought to prepare the way for still another blessing.

The success of the plan at first may depend partly on having an inconspicuous entrance. Especially in a village or small town,

194

the average person does not care to be seen going in to consult a specialist in disorders of the soul. The watchful neighbor might whisper, " What has Mary Small been doing now? " The same principle applies to the work of an attorney. In a recent book, *Country Lawyer,*[1] Bellamy Partridge explains about his first office: " People do not want others to know when they are consulting a lawyer, and there was absolutely no privacy about the iron staircase. Anybody climbing those ornamental cast-iron stairs was going to a law office. There was absolutely no other place to go." When the young attorney moved, his practice picked up.

The time of day also needs to be chosen with care. It should not conflict with the customary hour for holding a funeral. The time for seeing the minister ought to suit the convenience of the persons he is trying to reach. The constituency varies from one parish to another. The most common hour seems to be after the midday meal. Such appointments by day seem preferable to those after sundown; the sunlight suggests the opening up of the heart. For much the same reason one does not employ the name " office hours," as that would sound professional, not spiritual.

Like anything else in a man's work, the pastor's hour does not work automatically. The place and the time need to be kept before the people. When once the announcement has been made, the appointment should be kept, day after day. The persons who will respond tend to be sensitive. If once a shrinking inquirer finds the door of the study locked at a time when he has been asked to come, he will probably never return. At first there may be no callers. Hence there ought to be on hand certain reading or writing that needs to be done. It would not be wise for a busy layman to find the servant of the Lord twiddling his thumbs and wondering how to put in the time until a caller appeared.

2. *The Advantages of the Plan.* If people form the habit of coming, the plan affords distinct advantages. It enables the minister to confer individually with friends whom he might

not find at home if he called. The fact that the other person takes the initiative shows that there need be no " psychological approach." Other things being equal, the pastor is able to accomplish more in an hour by sitting still than when he goes from house to house. That other sort of calling, however, proves needful, in addition to the pastor's hour. The majority of those whom he ought to see will not come to the study.

The purpose is much the same as in a pastoral call. The subject of conversation, however, may be more specific. Here only one person at a time meets the clergyman. Ideally, there should be only a single matter for discussion. Actually, it takes time and talk before many a visitor arrives at the root of the matter. All of this procedure may seem to be " new," but it is so merely in terminology and in outer appearances. Back in 1859, when George Eliot wrote *Adam Bede,* did not Mr. Irwine, the genial rector, encourage the young nobleman, Arthur Donnithorne, to open up his heart and confess how he had dealt with Hetty? Did not the two men face each other across a table, and did not the clergyman follow the " technique " that we call modern? In the history of the Church almost every parish minister with a shepherd heart has had some sort of pastor's hour.

In the Protestant Church, however, the custom is beginning to take on new forms. A recent graduate of a seminary, perhaps twenty-seven years young, and unmarried, has had printed for free distribution a four-page leaflet entitled *Pastoral Services.* He does not suggest any particular hour but holds himself free for appointments. On the second page the list of nineteen representative problems to be solved includes the following:

" Difficulties for you and your family, created by the war ";
" Misunderstanding between husband and wife ";
" How to . . . help a child who constantly gets into mischief ";
" Planning a . . . way of life for older people ";
" Worry about physical or mental illness ";
" Difficulty in getting or keeping a job ";
" Difficulties in understanding the Bible."

On the third page this is the leading paragraph: " You will be able to consult with an ordained Minister of the Gospel, a man of God, with professional training and experience. He knows spiritual powers, as well as community resources, and is equipped to help you find a way to work things out. His understanding and suggestions, together with your own efforts and the help of God, may bring about a real solution of your problem."

That seems to put the Almighty in an advisory capacity. However, on the first page and the last the clergyman shows that his ministry aims to be Christ-centered. The young man is doing a good work, and he will grow. Nevertheless, his claims seem to be sweeping. Some of us who have had many times as much experience would be more cautious about committing ourselves. " Let not him that girdeth on his armor boast himself as he that putteth it off " (I Kings 20:11b).

3. *The Arguments Against the Plan.* Why do some spiritually-minded ministers and laymen still look askance at the pastor's hour? Perhaps because it tends to mechanize and standardize what should remain personal and vital. More probably, this " new " way of working may lead to dependence on psychology instead of on God. There may also be undue stress on sex. If certain advocates of personal counseling follow the teachings that appear in their books, matters of sex loom large. Then too the pastor's hour adds that much more to his burdens and cares. If people come, the strain will tell. If they do not, why pretend to have what does not exist?

The real difficulty may be that the minister does not know how to help one person after another in quest of heart's ease. Before any minister sets apart a special hour for soul surgery, he ought to have had signal success as a pastor. After he has learned how to excel in the cure of souls, he can begin to consider the wisdom of devoting to his specialty an hour a day, five days in the week.

However skilled the pastoral counselor, the plan works better in a vast city than in a village parish. Many people like to confide in a comparative stranger. Once while the author was holding meetings in a city far from home a young woman made an appointment to meet him late in the afternoon. Without delving unduly into details she made clear that she had been going about at night with an older man whom she knew to be married. After several consultations she outlined a procedure that she began to follow. It included a penitent approach to the man's wife, who knew the facts. Thus the younger woman found peace with God and herself. Further into the mess one need not go just now. Later when she wrote about the outcome she said quite frankly: " One reason I came was that I knew you were a stranger. I do not wish to meet every day on the street the minister to whom I have opened up my heart. He might talk in his sleep and tell his wife about my sins."

In view of what some ministers are doing, by way of experiment, let it be clear that pastoral counseling depends on Christian truth, not modern psychology. Psychology relates to method, not spiritual power. Many laymen dread present-day psychology. Even if they did not, they would wish it to be administered by an expert. After having enjoyed a few entertaining lectures, no surgeon of the soul should attempt to employ the methods of the medically trained psychiatrist.

However it be in a vast city, and in a huge church, the average minister cannot afford to alienate local physicians. As Cabot and Dicks remind us, doctors do not even like to have ministers talk much in the technical terms of the medical world. Still more frankly these two specialists tell us: " Don't practice psychotherapy in any technical sense (or so that the patient or the doctor knows it). Come as a friend or as a minister and not as a healer; then you will get on well with doctors. They fear competition and interference, in church clinics or home visits." [2]

These experts likewise warn us not to use in the pulpit the findings of the consulting room. Naturally some people relish an account of that suicide over in an Ohio town, or that sex tangle out in Oregon. But what right has the minister of the Gospel to drag family skeletons from the closet and dangle

them before strangers? To be sure more than one metropolitan preacher does so, apparently with impunity. Such a ten-
talent man may be a law to himself. Many of his methods would
not work in a parish with a stable constituency. Perhaps for
this reason it is unfortunate that young ministers choose their
models among men with something akin to genius. Cow Creek
still differs from New York City. Thank God! [3]

4. The Method of Procedure. In spite of the warnings
written above, the author believes in personal counseling by
the local pastor who excels as a physician of the soul. As in
home visiting, there can be no fixed " technique." One cannot
learn the fine art by reading a few books (including this one!)
and listening to lectures. Neither can one watch an expert at
work. How could he deal rightly with a quivering soul if a
third person were present? As an Irish student might say,
" How can I be with him when he is alone with the patient? "

The pastor's hour calls for insight and perseverance, as well
as gentleness and mercy. The spirit of the minister ought to be
like that of the Master. " He knew what was in man." These
words in the Fourth Gospel (John 2:25b) appear just before
the record of His dealings with Nicodemus and with the
woman at the well. According to Dean W. L. Sperry, of the
Harvard Divinity School, " As we turn the pages of the Gospels we have the strange feeling that we are in the presence of
Someone who understands us. The hold of such a Person over
us is strange and strong. To be known is in some ways a deeper
experience than to know." [4]

A pastoral counselor makes the other person feel at home in
the study. The caller should say to himself: " This man is my
friend. He cares for me personally. He will do all he can to
help me." In much the same spirit a wise professor in the medical school told a young doctor who inquired about developing
a bedside manner, " Get interested in your patient and your
bedside manner will take care of itself." The surest way for a
pastor to show such an interest is to let the other person talk.
Then the minister listens with eyes fixed on the other person's

face. Occasionally, however, when the disclosure bids fair to become painful, it may be better to look elsewhere, though without seeming startled or bored.

During the conversation it should seldom prove necessary to take notes. Once in a while it may be wise to jot down a statement of fact. If the minister promises to make a call, or if he asks for a later interview, that should be written down at once, and perhaps confirmed by oral repetition. In other respects the account of what occurs ought to be written down after the friend has departed. Then the notes should be filed where they will be accessible to the pastor before this friend calls again.

At length the time will come for the call to end. It may last thirty minutes, or even longer. If a minister sets apart an hour a day, five days in the week, he can count on seeing perhaps ten persons between Sundays. If there is a secretary she can make such appointments by telephone or in person. Even at such a slow rate, the pastor must guard every minute, lest he keep busy folk waiting unduly in the adjoining room. Like the specialist in medicine, the physician of the soul must learn to give the patient all the time and attention his case requires — and then close the call promptly. If another interview seems necessary, the minister can suggest a time in the near future, or else refer the matter to the secretary.

The call should end, normally, with a word from the Book, a brief prayer, and a benediction. As the friend is standing, ready to leave, the pastor should express his appreciation of the visit, and his assurance that God will guide in the solution of the problem. How and when the light will break, only the Lord can tell. It may be that the truth has already done its work in the waiting heart. If so, the friend can go forth in peace. The minister should thank God and take courage as he faces another person in quest of human sympathy and divine grace.

Suggested Readings

Blanton, Smiley, M.D., and Peale, Norman V., *Faith Is the Answer*. Abingdon-Cokesbury Press, 1940.

Cameron, William A., *The Clinic of a Cleric*. Harper & Brothers, 1931.

Dicks, Russell L., *Pastoral Work and Personal Counseling*. The Macmillan Company, 1944.

Gray, A. Herbert, *About People*. Charles Scribner's Sons, 1934.

May, Rollo, *The Art of Counseling*. Abingdon-Cokesbury Press, 1939.

Personal Counseling: A Bibliography. Federal Council of the Churches of Christ in America, 1943 (5 cents).

XXV

The Servant of the Community

WHAT should be the attitude of the minister toward the local community? The answer lies somewhere between two extremes. A clergyman of a certain type makes three hundred addresses a year outside his parish. Needless to say, he neglects the flock. Another pastor acts as though he were not concerned about the community. Even in a downtown church, he may have no influence beyond his congregation. Whether he follows after John Wesley or John Calvin, Charles H. Spurgeon or Phillips Brooks, that way of living seems shortsighted and selfish, if not unchristian. "I look upon all the world as my parish."

1. *The Pastor in the Community.* A man's influence depends partly on the size and character of the city or town. A well-known clergyman moved to a large residential church in Pittsburgh. He had been pastor of a smaller congregation in a county seat town of Ohio. There he had spoken in every township. He had met outside his church practically every man in the county. In all sorts of civic affairs, directly and indirectly, he had made his influence felt for righteousness and progress. In the much larger city parish he found no such opportunity. Only the exceptional minister of a residential community church can make a strong impression outside his own neighborhood.

Whatever the field, the pastor should evince a hearty concern for everything that tends to make the community better. He should visit the principal of schools, make friends with the city librarians, promote the maintenance of playgrounds, and do everything else to show that he wishes the community to become a worthy abode for God's little boys and girls. Especially should the clergyman establish friendly relations with the city editor of each paper — or perhaps the church editor. The same applies to the civic officials in his part of the city or county. If the minister wishes to discuss any civic matter that seems to involve criticism, let him go in person. If he has anything in the way of commendation, he should write. He would be amazed to learn how few letters of thanks city officials and newspaper men receive, and how many " knocks."

These men in public life soon appraise any clergyman who attracts their attention. They find in him either a helper in promoting every worthy cause, or a parasite who insists on receiving favors but never renders the community an unselfish service. If all this sounds extreme, cultivate the friendship of a city editor. Someday invite him out to lunch, or dinner, whichever will not come during the rush hour. Ask in confidence about his experiences with Protestant clergymen. He will probably report that Roman Catholics do such things more wisely. They plan all their work, which includes securing free publicity in the papers.

The pastor should also be a good churchman. As such, he ought to fulfill his obligations to his branch of the Ecumenical Church. He should likewise show himself friendly with other congregations and their ministers. Except in a large city, he ought to call on every incoming pastor. If that proves too much of an undertaking, he can write a friendly letter of welcome. He should likewise show a hearty concern for such associations as the Y.M.C.A., the Y.W.C.A., and the Red Cross.

For an example of community influence, turn to Charles Kingsley. At the age of fifty, he became canon of the cathedral at Chester, England. " A few days after his arrival Kingsley took the chair at a meeting of the Archeological Society. There he expressed a desire to put himself ' at the service of the good citizens of Chester,' and those ' good citizens ' took him to their hearts at once." In one or the other of two weekly newspapers at Chester, almost every issue contained a column or more from Kingsley. At times he would prepare the " leader." He spoke at all sorts of civic gatherings, and he excelled in distributing

prizes at school celebrations. In countless ways he exercised a
salutary influence over the life of his home city. For instance,
he found young shopmen and clerks who lacked cultural advantages. He gathered them together in a school that later developed into the Chester Natural Science Society, with three
hundred and fifty members. Is it any wonder that the biographer names one of her chapters " At the Service of the Good
Citizens of Chester "? [1]

2. *The Limits of Community Service.* It would scarcely
be wise for many a pastor to take Charles Kingsley as a model.
He was a man of unusual ability, and he had reached the age
of fifty years. He had learned how to engage in extraparochial
activities without neglecting his study or pastoral work. While
realizing the value of such widespread service, the average pastor can safely content himself with a more restricted program.
In response to appeals for outside activity, more or less secular,
he can say with a wise religious leader of old, " I am doing a
great work, so that I cannot come down: why should the work
cease, whilst I leave it, and come down to you? " (Neh. 6:3).

Many a clergyman these days seems to be dissipating his en-
ergies. In the seminary he was not able to form habits of system and concentration. He tried to do more different things
than the Lord requires of any man in twenty-four hours. Consequently he may never have learned to do any one thing well,
or long at a time. His people say that his pulpit work has become thin. His personality has not grown rich and strong.
Every once in a while he feels obliged to go away from home
to be spiritually " charged," whereas he ought to be a self-
starter.

Except during the midsummer vacation it is a wise rule to
remain at home on the Lord's Day and five days every week.
It is prudent to accept outside speaking invitations only when
they do not interfere with the routine work of the parish. Once
a week for an outside address might serve as the upper limit.
Except for meetings of Church bodies, which one attends as
a representative of the congregation, it should not be necessary

to take time from pastoral calling to hear anyone talk. When a Presbyterian minister in Pittsburgh reproached a Lutheran pastor for not attending a midwinter conference, the latter replied, " Pardon me, sir, I am at work this afternoon in the hospitals seeing the kind of people you are always too busy to visit." Yet we wonder why the Lutheran Church is growing.

As for civic service, why not do much of it indirectly? In these days almost every parish includes a number of elderly men who have retired. Such laymen need to have their horizons broadened by helping on social welfare committees. Think of the work such men have been doing on the Rationing Board. The Lord never intended that ministers alone should engage in benevolent activities. Let the pastor delegate such privileges. Especially with the aid of the women, a wise minister can meet almost every social need indirectly.

These counsels have to do with the clergyman who is fairly young. For the first five years, or even ten, let him concentrate. After that he may find it feasible to branch out. Meanwhile his habits of study and calling should have become fixed. Then he will find joy in putting first the one thing given him to do: to promote the Kingdom of God by building up the local church.

Listen to a strong man of yesterday, Charles E. Jefferson: " Keep your local church at the center of your world. . . . The work of the preacher is with his church; the work of the church is with the world. Let the preacher concentrate himself upon his church, and his church will take hold of the town, the nation, and the nations. Ministers who rush hither and thither, eaten up with reformatory zeal, meddling with this and dabbling with that, do not begin to do so much for the advancement of the Kingdom as do the men who stay at home and pour out into the souls of their own people the full measure of their vitality and devotion." [2]

For much the same ideal turn to Canon Peter Green, of Manchester. Like C. E. Jefferson, Canon Green has built up a strong downtown church composed largely of stalwart men. Listen

to his working philosophy: " The layman wants his clergyman
to be, not his equal in matters of this world, but his superior
and guide in matters of the world to come." " If a man is wholly
set on his work, and makes it the chief object and delight of his
life, he will not be likely to give too much time to things not
connected with it." [3] As for various forms of amusement, not
wrong in themselves, Canon Green reports that laymen wonder
how the minister can have so much free time for pursuits not
connected with their lifework. In short, let the clergyman be a
clergyman!

Suggested Readings

Green, Peter, *The Man of God*. Hodder & Stoughton, Ltd., 1935.
Green, Peter, *The Town Parson*. London, 1919.

XXVl

The Work of a Paid Assistant

" How can one do all this pastoral work single-handed? " In a church with five hundred members or more, there should be a full-time secretary, as well as a sexton. Otherwise the minister might become an executive, instead of a pastor and a prophet. In a congregation of a thousand or more, there should also be an assistant pastor. With every increase of five hundred members, there ought to be an additional full-time worker. Of course these figures must be arbitrary. They simply state the need of expert help. Let us think of a church with a thousand members.

1. *Securing the Assistant.* As in training a husband, it is necessary first to lay hands on the mortal. Whatever the state of the times, it may prove hard to find a suitable assistant. In days of depression the church officers may have difficulty in paying the present workers promptly each month. In soft and easy times there may be enough money in hand but it may prove impossible to secure the proper workers. At present the demand for young ministerial assistants far exceeds the supply. After World War II the reverse may be true.

The exceptional city pastor, however, experiences no insuperable difficulty. From year to year he supervises two or three strong young men, fully ordained. In the past he has had rare success as a trainer of ministers for strategic posts. Whenever a vacancy occurs on his ministerial staff, more than one strong youth stands ready to fill the vacant place. Such a senior pastor may have earned the reputation of working his helpers hard, but fairly. Thus he prepares each of them for independent service. One reason for his record is that in the beginning he makes this fact clear: he engages an assistant pastor, not a rival preacher. Dr. B. C. Clausen once wrote, " I wanted an assistant pastor who had no ambition to preach me out of my pulpit! "

Occasionally there comes a call for a man to serve as the junior " preacher." Over in Edinburgh, Alexander Whyte sent forth a succession of able young men, each of whom had shared in the pulpit work at Free St. George's. Every one of those men became a power for God, each in a fashion all his own. In the normal parish, however, the officials expect the senior minister to do the pulpit work. What they desire is someone to share the pastoral labors.

For this sort of routine drudgery the assistant may feel something akin to distaste. Has he not dreamed of the hour when he will be ordained? Then he will come into his own as a master of assemblies. Down in his heart he may feel sure that he preaches better than the older man, who has a simple way of appealing to childlike people. Erelong some of the congregation may begin to agree with the young man's appraisal. Hence they feed his vanity. After a while the senior pastor may report that the young minister excels nowhere except in the pulpit. When the parting comes, each of the two ministers " reluctantly acquiesces."

Such tension may spring partly from a lack of clear understanding at the start. Over at Carr's Lane in Birmingham, Robert William Dale used to insist that the senior minister be frank. Dale had served both as a young assistant and as a senior pastor. In terms of the American scene, there might be a formal contract between the young man and the official board. In it they would prescribe his duties. Somehow they would make clear that he is not to serve as the errand boy of the Ladies' Aid Society or as the prospective successor to the present " preacher." In short, let the young man come as an assistant " pastor." Is he not a " ministering shepherd "? That means a servant of God who tends the sheep.

Sometimes the seminary graduate assumes oversight of the young people's work. If he has personality and charm, he can win a following among the young folk and their friends. Thus he may widen the gulf between the two generations. As in Corinth, some may keep saying, "I am of Paul." Others insist, "We prefer Apollos." Perhaps they mean "Apollo"! The ladies insist that the young assistant looks like a Greek god. They forget that Apollo is said to have served as a tender of sheep. That scarcely describes an armchair supervisor of programs, who ought to be at work with people out in the parish.

Any young minister should welcome an opportunity to engage in pastoral work under an experienced coach. What does the seminary graduate need so much as the insight that comes through entering home after home? There he can learn how to deal with all sorts of people. Even if he were mature enough to qualify as an expert in young people's work — which proves to be unexpectedly difficult — would that be ideal for them or for him? In ten or fifteen years he will seem too old for that kind of service. After he has lost his youthful spirits, what will he do the rest of his days? As for the young people, the modern fashion of herding them off by themselves does not appear to have worked so well as the advocates used to predict. Why not let the assistant deal somewhat with sick folk, as well as shut-in friends, and allow the mature pastor time to show his heart's concern for the young people?

Unfortunately, it may require two or three years to train a novice in pastoral work. By that time he has begun to desire a field of his own. Consequently, there is a growing feeling that the church of tomorrow may have to depend largely on full-time lay assistants of mature years, or on consecrated women, specially trained. Apart from the ever-present possibility that the lady assistant will marry, she may be worth twice as much as an inexperienced seminary graduate, however brilliant. Especially in work among women and children, her gifts and graces supplement those of the pastor.

A congregation may solve part of this problem by securing a talented layman who has retired from teaching or business. At Princeton University the head of an important department recently told a few friends that down in his heart he has always wished to become a parish minister. Up in Boston a retired university professor renders full-time service in the congregation where he formerly took an active part on the official board. During the present shortage of ministers who have sufficient caliber to forge ahead in difficult fields, why not keep on the watch for the consecrated layman?

Meantime two movements offer promise. One is the Lutheran plan of a year's " internship " for the seminary student after he has completed the second year of study. Not having been ordained, he should know that he serves in a subordinate capacity. If he works under a leader with vision and tolerance, the young man should come back to the seminary with a new vision of serving God as a pastor. At present the supply of young men for internships does not begin to meet the demand. After times again become normal, if they ever do, this plan should be far more widely employed. Then there will arise a generation of ministers with shepherd hearts.

The other movement concerns young women. If they are to become assistant " pastors," rather than church secretaries, they need special training. In the best sense their " professional " schooling ought to be " functional." It should prepare each of them to become a " pastor " among women and girls, as well as little boys. Especially should it make a woman skillful and eager in serving as a friendly counselor. She ought to help anyone whom the pastor sends for the aid that comes from God through a Christian woman with charm and skill. In terms of the present book, a worker of this kind ought to excel in every sphere except that of " attracting the men." Even there she may prove adept, but only with one!

2. *Serving as an Assistant.* With some exceptions, the readers of this volume may serve as assistants, not as senior pastors. Any mature minister who wishes to train young helpers ought to read *The Life of Chevalier Jackson.*[1] That wizard in making and using the bronchoscope has given detailed suggestions on how to train an assistant. Here are some of the ideas: Do not keep him under, or browbeat him. Encourage

him. Let him learn on easy cases, not those that may prove fatal. Get him to report his cases before a medical society. Be present, and tell about the good work he has done. After a while send him out to a practice of his own. In short, follow the Golden Rule.

As for the assistant, let him learn humility. In the language of the Apostle Peter, as translated by James Moffatt, the young man should " put on the apron of humility to serve " (I Peter 5:5). Venerable Peter must have been thinking of a scene long before. In the Upper Room, he and other " seminary students " had been unwilling to engage in menial tasks. Hence the Lord had set them an example. Peter's later words about humility appear in close connection with his injunctions to render inconspicuous " pastoral " service. In like manner, the Apostle Paul told his friends from Ephesus that he had labored there as a pastor: " Serving the Lord with all humility . . . I . . . taught you publickly, and from house to house " (Acts 20:19, 20).

The work of the assistant shepherd likewise calls for adaptability. In the seminary the young man may have thought of himself as about to be engaged in gigantic enterprises for saving the world wholesale. Now he finds that he must learn how to get along with all sorts of human beings, one by one. Somehow he must adapt his sweeping generalizations to the needs of a pious old German woman whose heart has been broken by an awful war. Despite the recent craze for young leaders, he must serve under a mature pastor who knows that God loves aged saints. In short, as in matrimony, being an assistant calls for countless adjustments, and for team play.

Above all should there be a spirit of loyalty. According to a book that every minister should prize,[2] loyalty means " the willing and practical and thoroughgoing devotion of a person to a cause," as that cause is embodied in a person with authority to lead. For the assistant pastor the supreme cause should be the Kingdom, as represented in the local church. The leader to whom he should prove loyal is the senior pastor. Before entering the field the young man should assure himself about the fitness of the one who is to serve as coach. Once the relation has begun, let the young man live and learn in the spirit of loyalty and love.

Where such a spirit reigns, the people in a large congregation can enjoy as good pastoral care as though there were only two or three hundred members. That may be enough to keep one man busy. Meanwhile the most pressing problems of the average congregation seem to be pastoral. If in the next few years we can train a generation of young ministers with shepherd hearts, we shall soon have more of " peace and prosperity " among Protestant churches. One of the very best ways to secure such training is to serve two or three years under a strong, kind " ministering shepherd."

XXVII

The Enlisting of Lay Visitors

THE pastor of a church with a thousand members recently told the official board, " Your offer to provide an assistant minister cheers me, but I prefer to follow the present plan of letting the women do the calling." If every man in such a position were gifted in getting women to enjoy intensive visitation, there might not be so many complaints about the difficulty of securing and retaining pastoral assistants. Whatever the number and the skill of the salaried workers, there ought to be much calling by the women, as well as by the men. Let us begin with the laymen. How can one lead them to engage in calling?

1. *Visiting by the Men.* In many a local church the people complain that they never see a lay officer of the church at their homes unless he comes for money. On the other hand, a leading churchman in Hagerstown, Maryland, recently told about the most memorable experiences in all his life. Years before, he had served as one of fifty elders in our Central Church of Buffalo, New York. There he had charge of a district comprising fifty members. At his election he understood that he was to call on every family, or isolated member, prior to each quarterly Communion. Evidently he regarded himself as a lay shepherd. Twenty-five years later he looked back on those pastoral ministries with gladness of heart. Why should such an experience prove exceptional? What are lay officers of the church elected to do if not to care for the sheep?

In our branch of the Church the deacons often wonder what they are supposed to do. As Billy Sunday used to say, they ought to " deak." Among other things worthy, they should be tireless in visiting the sick and the needy. No one of them may have much time to spare during the week. But if they apportion such work, fifteen or twenty deacons can accomplish

a vast deal for God. In one parish they found that a working
girl in the congregation was unable to defray the cost of her
mother's operation. They helped her with the other expenses,
and then they approached the surgeon. When they offered to
pay the bill if he would divide it in two, he declined, absolutely. He took the statement and smilingly tore it in pieces.
Again one asks, why should such lay services appear exceptional?

Some of the more tactful men should find joy in calling on
convalescents, shut-in folk, and those in sorrow. The same
holds true even more largely in evangelism. Ofttimes the right
lay worker can do personal work better than the minister. At
least the layman and the pastor can engage in teamwork.
Among the unused resources of the typical church, none seems
quite so promising as the man power among the laymen. Here
and there one finds a congregation that deserves to be called
" a men's church." The pastor who knows how to inspire laymen to become visitors can borrow an ancient battle song:

> " For that the leaders took the lead in Israel,
>   For that the people offered themselves willingly;
>   Bless ye the Lord. . . .
> " My heart is toward the governors of Israel,
>   That offered themselves willingly among the people:
>   Bless ye the Lord " (Judg. 5:2, 9).

2. Calling by Husband and Wife. Ordinarily lay workers accomplish more when each one goes out alone than when
they visit by pairs. In calling on newcomers, however, a husband and wife can present the claims of the church more per-
suasively together than if they went separately. The same principle often obtains in home evangelism. The value of the plan
depends largely on choosing the right two. Not every earnest
couple knows how to present the claims of Christ and the
home church in a social call. On the other hand, the minister
who becomes skillful in choosing lay helpers can increase his
usefulness manyfold. He can also prolong his life. If he attempted to do everything himself, he might shorten his earthly
career. At least he would fill his days with futility and despair.

A word of warning may prove needful for the novice. Never call publicly for volunteers to engage in a delicate task. Once when young and callow the writer was asked to announce from the pulpit that the junior department of the Church School needed a certain number of teachers. Out of a throng that filled the spacious sanctuary, only two persons responded. Both of them had begun to grow old, and each had become deaf. Even with an old-fashioned ear trumpet, it was a wonder that either had heard the minister's plea. If such willing workers had tried to teach a group of boisterous boys or giggling girls, what would the latter not have dropped down into those yawning cornucopias? As with new converts, church callers must be hand-picked, by one who knows how.

Former Dean Charles R. Brown reports [1] a case that shows how an experienced pastor can use a husband and wife in parish calling. To this minister came a woman with a breaking heart. To him as a stranger she confided a tale of approaching desertion by her husband, who had hitherto seemed faithful. The clergyman listened attentively. After a while he led in prayer. Telling the visitor frankly that he did not yet know what to do, he asked her to mention the matter to no one else, and to keep on praying. After she had gone, he himself looked to God, more than seven times. At last he saw the light. Then he determined to rely on friendly visitation by a number of attractive couples.

The pastor did not tell these friends why he wished them to call. He simply advised each couple to make friends with the husband and wife, and show concern for their two children. One pair of lay visitors went to the home on Monday evening, another couple on Tuesday, and so on through Friday. Meanwhile the minister kept praying, and so did the tremulous wife. Before the week had ended, her husband broke down and confessed what he had planned to do. Then he volunteered to make any possible reparation. The way to do that, even in part, called for powers higher than his own.

On Sunday morning the penitent husband asked her if they could attend church together. In the sanctuary those two stray

sheep doubtless found their way into the fold of God. Such
a happy ending leads one to ask: Could not many a household
tragedy be averted if every community had such a leader and
such visitors? As the lawyers often tell us, " Cases are won in
chambers, not in court." All the while there can be no cheap
and easy way of dealing with such a human problem in a
non-Christian home.

3. *Visiting by the Women.* In spreading the Gospel of
good will and friendliness, young people can take part. So can
boys and girls. If Sherlock Holmes, or one of John Buchan's
heroes, could use small lads in undercover work, how much
more can the Christian pastor employ a ten- or twelve-year-
old boy or girl to gain an entrance into many a home. All the
while, every pastor knows that the best visitors emerge among
women. They have more time than men. Women also use more
tact.

A case will show lack of tact on the part of a well-meaning
man. At the suggestion of the pastor this officer went to call
on a man who had suffered two attacks of angina pectoris. The
minister had advised the caller to keep away from that subject, but the layman suffered a lapse of memory. He tried to
entertain the invalid by recounting case after case of men
about the same age who had succumbed to angina pectoris. No
woman gifted as a caller would ever commit such a series of
blunders.

The writer has known more than one congregation where
the climate has been changed by friendly visiting by God's
gentlewomen. Once the atmosphere of the parish made a newcomer think of " Greenland's icy mountains." Now one feels
prompted to sing: " Fair are the meadows, fairer still the wood-
lands, robed in the blooming garb of spring." The transformation begins when the local church ceases to be a preaching station and becomes a family circle of the redeemed. People begin
really to know and love one another. Then they rejoice in all
the ties that bind them together in the service of God.

In a certain parish " the flower lady " used to be counted

the most useful member. Every weekday, after she had done her work at home, she gave herself to a ministry of love among the sick, the sorrowing, and the shut-in friends. More than anyone else in the parish, she kept the minister informed about homes where his presence seemed desirable. He in turn let her know where a ministry of " sweetness and light " would do most for the cause they both loved. Eternity alone will reveal how much good one woman of this kind accomplishes by using flowers in gaining access to homes and hearts that need sunshine from the throne.

A woman of a different sort used to serve as an unpaid assistant to the pastor. At first she had not understood him, and she had told him exactly what she thought. Later she tried to make amends by going about over the parish doing good. Fortunately, she could spare almost every afternoon. Since she owned an automobile, and could secure the help of other women, she reached almost as many homes as the pastor. Once when he received a summons to minister down in the red-light district, she learned about the matter after his first visit. Then she insisted on taking the case out of his hands. Needless to say, she handled it better than he could have done. Who can deal with a fallen girl so well as a woman who stands ready to act as her mother in the Lord?

When the pastor enlists the help of worthy women in sufficient numbers, the spiritual life of the congregation becomes quickened. Strange to tell, no new machinery may prove needful. In three different parishes the writer found organized groups of women who needed such an outlet. Instead of serving all afternoon in the same sort of duties as fell to their lot at home — preparing meals and planning for further good things to eat — those lovers of Christ and the home church found joy in calling throughout the community. If any minister longs to witness in the home parish a sort of continuous revival, let him enthuse the right sort of women as the assistant pastors, in the name of the Good Shepherd.

4. Visiting in a Large Congregation. In an occasional city

parish it may prove necessary to organize these church visitors,
separately. For example, take " The Women's Guild " of the
Madison Avenue Presbyterian Church in New York City. Last
year the officers reported 2,939 members, many of whom re-
sided in tenement houses on the East Side. Under the friendly
oversight of Mrs. George A. Buttrick, wife of a pastor, more
than forty " church visitors " go in and out of countless homes.
The character of the work appears in a sixteen-page booklet,
neatly printed, and bound in stiff paper. From this little manual the writer has learned more about the way good women
should engage in friendly calling than from half a dozen books
full of hifalutin theories. These are excerpts from the booklet:

" The Church Visitors supplement the work of the Ministers." [The church staff includes three full-time ordained
clergymen.] " In our large and varied parish it is impossible
for the ministers to call on every family as frequently or regularly as is often necessary, or to meet adequately the needs
apparent in so many homes. The work of the Church Visitors
is therefore a pastoral service, and theirs is a position of trust
and responsibility." [In what follows note the stress on the
singular.]

The Church Visitor will " clothe her identity in that of the
Church "; " approach each family with courtesy "; " develop
a keen observation "; " learn quietly and appreciatively to listen "; " resist the temptation to assume the parents' task of
running the home, or of solving its problems "; " learn to sus-
pend judgment in situations other than those of acute emergency "; and above all, " cultivate patience." " The Visitor,
as we have said, is the Visitor from the Church." " There is a
way of life that Christ has taught and Himself lived, a strength
that comes of private prayer, a knowledge born of study, and
a force generated by corporate worship." " These emphases
must not be forgotten in the cry for material help." [The congregation also carries on an intensive program of social welfare
work. What a practical commentary on Matt. 6:33!]

" *Frequency of Calls* (October 1st to June 1st) ": " On a

family financially sound and interested in the church, three or four calls "; " financially sound, but uninterested, although they send their children to the Church School, two calls until an increase in interest is apparent "; " financial instability, or chronic sickness, etc., a call every three or four weeks "; " an acute emergency, two or three calls close together until the emergency is over." " The Visitor is not asked to call regularly during the four summer months. It is suggested that she send an occasional letter or card." " Emergencies are handled during the summer by the Ministers or Lay Staff of the Church."

" The Visitor should report at once cases of sickness or sorrow where a call from a minister is advisable." " Where a family is out, the Visitor should leave the calling card provided." " The Visitor should refrain from giving her own address or telephone number. She is a Church Visitor. . . . The Family should be taught to ask for her at the Church, and look for her at its services. An occasional gift, — such as a book or a plant in times of sickness, — is allowable, but the Visitor should refrain from giving money, clothing, etc. Such gifts should be made only through the regular channels of the Church." " The Visitor is asked to see that her reports, written on the blanks provided, reach the Chairman each month." [Each report shows the number of calls made during the past month, and the names of the families visited. These records are entered in the permanent files of the Church.]

Even as condensed, what a statement about the title of the present chapter, " The Enlisting of Lay Visitors "! Where is the small congregation that shows more concern for its members, especially among the poor? Somehow or other, ministering shepherd, lead the good women to go and do likewise.

Suggested Reading

Fenn, Don F., *Parish Administration.* Morehouse-Gorham Company, Inc., 1938.

XXVIII

The Increase of Churchgoing

" A HOME-GOING pastor makes a churchgoing people." These words from Thomas Chalmers came out of his own experience. During the latter half of his life he stood forth as the mightiest of Presbyterian preachers and pastors. As a young clergyman Chalmers had accomplished almost nothing, either in pulpit or in parish. According to his son-in-law and biographer, " Parochial duties sat lightly upon Mr. Chalmers during the first seven years of his ministry at Kilmany [his first charge]. . . . It was only when specially invited to do so that he engaged in prayer. Two or three weeks annually were devoted to a visitation of his parish. . . . With the general body of his parishioners he had little intercourse.

" Upon the whole . . . Mr. Chalmers' ministry was unpopular and ineffective, his church but poorly attended, and his private ministrations followed with but trifling effects. But the great change came, and with it a total alteration in the discharge of all parochial duty. From a place of visible subordination, the spiritual care and cultivation of his parish was elevated to the place of clear and recognized supremacy. . . . [After a transforming illness] the first use he made of that returning strength . . . was to visit all the sick, the dying, and the bereaved in his parish. . . . A brief visit from him was often sufficient to shed a flood of light upon the understanding, or to pour a full tide of comfort into the heart." [1]

1. *The Effects of Pastoral Care.* From that time onward, in rural Kilmany and in downtown Glasgow, Chalmers excelled both as a preacher and as a pastor. In fact, any minister who is perplexed by the problem of caring for a large congregation in a vast unchurched area ought to study the methods of Thomas Chalmers. He relied largely on his men, the lay

officers. What should concern the average minister still more was the spirit of the pastor himself. At the height of his glory as the most commanding preacher of his day, Chalmers spoke about the sort of prestige he coveted: " The popularity of the heart [is] the only popularity that is worth the striving after — the popularity that is won in the bosom of families and at the side of deathbeds." [2]

What has all this to do with our " throng of churchgoing people? " Much every way! The decline in regular church attendance on the part of professing Christians has come during the years when pastoral calling has not been supreme in the daily life of many a parish minister. Here and there one finds a sanctuary filled with enthusiastic worshipers almost every Lord's Day. The pulpit work may not be of a high order. Whatever the defects, the preaching and the prayers help the people because they love and trust their pastor.

As a witness hear former Dean Charles R. Brown, of Yale. He is speaking after wide and varied observation: " The most successful ministers I have ever known, or known about, East and West, North and South, have been strong on pastoral visitation." Then he names certain giants of yesterday. " All of these men were active in calling upon their people. Would those churches have reached their large influence by any other method of pastoral care? Will someone be good enough to find me, in these days, strong, stable, growing, generous, spiritually-minded churches where no pastoral calling worth speaking of has been done in the last ten years? I do not know of any such." [3]

2. *The Varieties of Anemic Churches.* Under God, the progress of the Lord's work at home and abroad seems to depend chiefly on the state of religion in the parish church. With certain exceptions, that condition has not been gratifying. Recently in many quarters there seems to have been a forward movement, spiritually. Even so, there yet remains much land to be possessed before God will have His way in many a local church. How does He wish to remedy such a situation? Largely

through pastoral work. According to Chrysostom of old, " One man inspired with holy zeal sufficeth to amend an entire people."

Once again look at a few cases, thinly disguised. Recently a minister went into a divided church. Dearly did he love to preach, but soon he saw that he must win the hearts of the people in their homes. Ignoring both the vertical split under one predecessor, and the horizontal cleavage under another, the new minister went out to call and call and call. He surmised that one of the former pastors had been the worthy husband of a domineering wife, and that the other had mistaken his vocation; he might have succeeded as a purveyor of neighborhood news. With no regard to any previous state of warfare, the new minister went in and out among his people. Before long the sanctuary began to be filled. He did not draw them by his preaching, though he tried to feed them well whenever they appeared in the House of God.

Another pastor took the oversight of a disgruntled church. At first glance this case and the last one may seem parallel. In the field before us, however, the people had not quarreled with each other; they had lost confidence in the home church. They seemed to look on it as an entity apart from themselves. Many of them held aloof from public worship, and the offerings slumped. People kept moving to neighboring churches that could still " maintain the spiritual glow." Without calling attention to the anemic condition of the church body, the new minister began to call and call and call. Soon the people responded. In any normal field where this plan fails, there may be something wrong with the visiting.

A third minister went into a discouraged church. On every hand he heard the lament: " All the good people have moved away! If dear Doctor W. could not make the work go here, we might as well close our doors." Fortunately, the incoming pastor remembered another saying from Thomas Chalmers. One night he was standing on a bridge with a younger minister, Thomas Guthrie. Knowing that Guthrie felt appalled by the magnitude of his new undertaking in an ungodly neighbor-hood, Chalmers stretched forth his arm as though to pronounce the benediction on all the city homes. Then he spoke, with holy awe: " What a magnificent field of operations! " In the American city, also, the pastor in view found that God was waiting to bless the indefatigable labors of His undershepherd.

Once again, look at a deserted church. If the neighborhood has become depopulated, the doors of the sanctuary ought to be closed, reverently. However, they should be opened again as soon as the community becomes settled enough to need a district school. On the other hand, a church building practi-cally deserted may stand in the midst of teeming thousands. If unchurched and unsaved people live in the vicinity, who will say that the congregation has no chance to survive? At any rate, the leader ought to try the old-fashioned method of pastoral visiting.

Over in Dundee, Scotland, as late as March, 1939, people had almost ceased attending " Martyrs' Church." According to recent reports that House of God has since become a beehive of spiritual activity. The change has been wrought through prayer and household calling. " The minister with his wife and daughter began to visit the entire parish of 4,777 people [this does not mean church members], in tenements four or five stories high. . . . Within a year a hundred souls had been added to the church and the Sunday-evening service had grown from the smallest to the largest now worshipping in Dundee. The membership of the Sunday School had almost trebled, and the contributions to foreign missions had increased thirty-fold."

As a rule the results of parish visitation do not appear quickly, or seem striking. Rebuilding a congregation by visit-ing homes involves a vast deal of drudgery. The harvest may seem slow in appearing. Nevertheless, if the man of God works in a field where people are unchurched and unsaved, and if he enlists the right sort of lay visitors, he can count on an ingath-ering. In due season he shall reap if he faints not. Meanwhile let him keep on at work throughout the parish. Let him learn how to excel as a caller. " A home-going pastor makes a church-going people."

What parish minister does not long to become the pastor of a spiritual church, a friendly church, an active church? If so, why should any such clergyman think of moving to another field? All these ideals may become realities in a congregation with a home-going pastor. Church attendance may be only an index of spiritual health and growth. Even so, what " ministering shepherd " would not rejoice if his people could say to him at every Sunday morning service: " Now . . . are we all here present before God, to hear all things that are commanded thee of God " (Acts 10:33)?

That is the sort of expectant throng many a pastor faces from week to week. In a measure the same holds true at the evening service, or vespers. " Whatsoever a man soweth " in the way of pastoral calling, " that shall he also reap " in the form of enthusiastic church attendance.

Suggested Readings

Blackwood, Andrew W., *Evangelism in the Home Church,* Ch. VIII, " Parish Revival." Abingdon-Cokesbury Press, 1942.
Jefferson, Charles E., *The Building of the Church.* The Macmillan Company, 1913.

XXIX

The Rewards of Pastoral Work

" Who is the happiest man in town? " If you stop any friendly observer here at home and ask this question, he may think for a little while. Then he will say, " Our pastor." Each of our parish clergymen appears to excel as a shepherd, in a fashion all his own. That must be partly why these men look happy. If anyone takes a broader view in the history of the Church he will find that with few exceptions parish ministers have been radiant. In the service of the Good Shepherd and His sheep, such men have found joy as a by-product. During the discussion that follows, why not single out a typical pastor today? Let him serve as an example of all these truths.

1. *The Joys of a Healthy Body.* It is possible to be a good pastor when one is anemic, but that seems not to be the Lord's ideal. When the apostle declares, " I can do all things through Christ which strengtheneth me " (Phil. 4:13), he may refer partly to physical powers. Not only does pastoral work tax a man's physical resources, it likewise tends to make them larger. This may be why the hard-working pastor usually lives to a ripe old age. According to life insurance experts, the men of no other calling make such a record for longevity. Unlike many other busy men who retire, the pastor can look forward to a happy old age.

Physical well-being comes to the parish minister partly because of varied activities. Not even a family physician follows such a pleasing schedule from day to day. Think of long, quiet hours of study, other times for friendly contacts with people, one after another, and frequent opportunities for fellowship with groups of the best people in the community! What could do more to make a man happy and keep him well? Anyone who has tasted these pastoral joys, and then has moved into some restricted field of service, can understand why a pastor often gives thanks: " The lines are fallen unto me in pleasant places; yea, I have a goodly heritage " (Ps. 16:6).

Such work affords abundance of exercise in the open air. For a man who loves to call, there can be as much satisfaction in moving about over the parish as in a game of golf. That too has its place, but only as a diversion. In certain other lines of work men have to seek exercise apart from life's duties. All that the pastor need do is to plan his calling so as to use his muscles. Such was the report of a young pastor the other day. He had come to tell the professor about the first year on the field. The teacher had never seen the young man looking so well and so buoyant. In doing his work as a shepherd that minister had found fullness of joy and abundance of energy. He said that he wondered why some young clergymen seemed not to enjoy pastoral work.

2. *The Joys of a Healthy Soul.*   When the apostle wrote the following, perhaps he was addressing a young minister: " I wish above all things that thou mayest prosper and be in health, even as thy soul prospereth " (III John 2). Health of soul and haleness of body often go together. What, then, are the essentials for health of soul? Granting that the minister is alive and well, spiritually, how can he " maintain the spiritual glow "? That should come as the outshining of a heart aflame with love for God and for men.

Three things seem to be essential for spiritual health: food, fresh air, and exercise. In the Christian life we think of food as it is found chiefly in the Bible; of fresh air as it comes best on the mountaintop, where a man communes with his Lord; and of exercise as it comes through Christian service down in the valley. All of this appears in the daily routine of the pastor. Except during his midsummer holiday, he should never feel the need of going away from home to deepen and strengthen his spiritual life.

Think of the pastor's Bible. What an incentive the diligent shepherd has for searching the Scriptures! He must keep ever at hand something to help stray sheep. His rod and his staff may be the Bible and prayer. Often we have heard about the way a man should use the Scriptures in preparing to preach, or else engage in mission work. Someone should write a treatise about the pastor's need of searching the Bible every day so as to be ready for his parish ministry among men and women. A church-building program calls for a Bible-loving minister.

The same holds true with reference to prayer. In the homes of the people, and in the hospital, he prays often, though never long. When alone, he often carries to the mercy seat the burdens of those to whom he has listened during the day. Of course his intercessions should not be confined to his own parish. But that is where they ought to center. When he pleads for world-wide missions, or peace among the nations, how can he forget the bearing of such things on the church that he loves?

As for spiritual exercise, that comes to the pastor's soul every working day. Who else but a chaplain or a missionary has such abundant and fruitful opportunities to show the working values of the Christian religion? In fact, with the soul as with the body, all three ways of promoting health work together for good. In the pastor's everyday rounds he gains exercise that makes him hungry for the Book. That in turn leads him to relish the atmosphere of prayer. Is it any wonder that his heart keeps singing? He has a kind of soul-satisfying food that the world cannot give or take away. Such is the message of Matthew Arnold in his poem " East London." That is where one finds the slums of the English city.

> " 'Twas August, and the fierce sun overhead
>   Smote on the squalid streets of Bethnal Green,
>   And the pale weaver, through his windows seen
>   In Spitalfields, look'd thrice dispirited.
>
> " I met a preacher there I knew, and said:
>   ' Ill and o'erworked, how fare you in this scene? ' —
>   ' Bravely! ' said he; ' for I of late have been
>   Much cheer'd with thoughts of Christ, the living bread.' "

3. *The Joys of Serving Christ.*   The joy that the world cannot know comes to the worthy pastor. He brings to hungry hearts Jesus Christ, " the living bread." Under God, the parish minister is able to meet all sorts of human needs. In many hearts and homes he becomes " a friend that sticketh closer than a brother." He likewise goes forth in quest of the sheep that is lost. He spends himself for the weak and the helpless. He witnesses the transformation of weaklings into stalwart warriors, and of good people into still more glorious saints. He aids largely in building up the Kingdom of God at the home base, the local church. Who else on earth can taste such joys, unless it be the chaplain, or the missionary? Each of them like-wise serves as a shepherd of souls.

Many of us are working for God at second hand. The parish minister deals with the human problem at the source. That is in the hearts of men and women, one by one, and in their homes. The rest of us may seldom darken the threshold of a household in sorrow, or at a wedding feast. We may be doing our utmost to advance the interests of the Kingdom, but we work indirectly. According to John Bunyan, in *The Holy War,* the victory for God must be gained at the City of Mansoul. That calls for the work of the pastor. He must know how to enter through eye-gate as well as ear-gate. Somehow he should take possession of that citadel in the name of King Immanuel.

For a still more lofty view of the " ministering shepherd," turn to the Apostle Peter. Long before he began to be old, that impetuous disciple learned in theory how to obey the Chief Shepherd: " Feed my lambs "; " tend my sheep " (John 21:15, 16). Much later in a life of rare devotion Peter wrote his First Epistle. It shows that he had learned his lesson. This letter full of courage and hope sets forth the meaning and the glory of the God-serving pastor. Especially does the truth appear in the opening verses of the fifth chapter. There the apostle utters glowing words full of Christian hope: " When the chief Shepherd shall appear, ye shall receive a crown of glory that fadeth not away " (I Peter 5:4).

The man with the shepherd heart need not postpone his joys until the world to come. Every once in a while his heart should begin to glow afresh because a young man in the parish has gone into the ministry of the Gospel at home or abroad. Doubly joyful is the shepherd of souls when two or three of his sons follow in their father's footsteps. In our days of war and rebuilding who can hope to taste life's joys so fully as the young men whom God is calling to become preachers and pastors? May each of them, here and now, as in days to come, receive the benediction of the Covenant: —

" The God of peace, that brought again from the dead our Lord Jesus, that great shepherd of the sheep, through the blood of the everlasting covenant, make you perfect in every good work to do his will, working in you that which is wellpleasing in his sight, through Jesus Christ; to whom be glory for ever and ever. Amen " (Heb. 13:20, 21).

Suggested Reading

Jefferson, Charles E., *The Ministering Shepherd*. Hodder and Stoughton, 1912.

Appendix

BOOKS ABOUT PASTORAL WORK

THE dean of a famous medical school says that in order to know human nature a physician must read widely. The same holds true in the experience of a pastor. The literature in his field appears to be boundless. Much of it has already been mentioned in this volume. The following works indicate what sources a man ought to investigate if he wishes to engage in a special study. The first half of the list includes books about pastoral work. The latter half consists of biographies and autobiographies. The first is arranged chronologically; the second, alphabetically. Every pastor would enjoy the biographies.

Paul, The Pastoral Epistles.
Peter, The General Epistles.
Hermas (fl. 140), *The Shepherd of Hermas.*
Ambrose (340?-397), *On the Duties of the Clergy.*
Chrysostom (345?-407), *On the Priesthood.*
Gregory I (c. 540?-604), *The Pastoral Rule.*
Bernard of Clairvaux (1091-1153), *Tractatus de Moribus et Officiis Clericorum.*
Wycliffe, John (c. 1320?-1384), *Tractatus de Officio Pastorali.*
Langland, William, *The Vision of Piers Plowman* (1362).
Chaucer, Geoffrey, *The Canterbury Tales* (c. 1375-1393).
Luther, Martin, *The Table Talk.* Ed. by William Hazlitt (1895).
Hooker, Richard, *On the Laws of Ecclesiastical Polity* (1594-1618).
Herbert, George, *The Temple* (1631); *The Country Parson* (1652).
Andrewes, Lancelot, Bishop, *Manual of Private Devotions* (1648).
Taylor, Jeremy, *Holy Living* (1650); *Holy Dying* (1651).
Baxter, Richard, *The Reformed Pastor* (1656); *The Saints' Everlasting Rest* (1650).
Bunyan, John, *Grace Abounding* (1666); *The Pilgrim's Progress* (1678).
Goldsmith, Oliver, *The Vicar of Wakefield* (1766).
Wesley, John (1703-1791), *Journal.*
Cowper, William, " The Task " (1785).
Wordsworth, William, " The Excursion," Bks. V, VIII (1814).

Keble, John, *The Christian Year* (1827).
Chalmers, Thomas, *The Parochial System* (1852).
Trollope, Anthony, *The Warden* (1855); *Barchester Towers* (1857).
Stowe, Harriet Beecher, *The Minister's Wooing* (1859).
Hugo, Victor, *Les Misérables* (1862).
Macdonald, George, *David Elginbrod* (1863); *et al.*
Eliot, George (Marian Evans), *Scenes from Clerical Life* (1858); *Romola* (1863).
Oliphant, Margaret, *The Rector* (1863); *The Perpetual Curate* (1864).
Newman, John Henry, *Apologia pro Vita Sua* (1864).
Ward, Mrs. Humphry, *Robert Elsmere* (1888).
Barrie, Sir James M., *Auld Licht Idylls* (1888); *The Little Minister* (1891).
Deland, Margaret W., *John Ward, Preacher* (1888); *Dr. Lavendar's People* (1904).
Crockett, Samuel R., *The Stickit Minister* (1893).
Watson, John (Ian Maclaren), *Beside the Bonnie Brier Bush* (1894).
Connor, Ralph (Charles W. Gordon), *Black Rock* (1898); *The Sky Pilot* (1899); *The Sky Pilot in No Man's Land* (1919).
King, Basil, *The Lifted Veil* (1919).
Walpole, Hugh, *The Cathedral* (1922).
Lewis, Sinclair, *Elmer Gantry* (1927).
Cronin, A. J., *The Keys of the Kingdom* (1941).
Douglas, Lloyd C., *The Robe* (1942); *Green Light* (1935); *et al.*
Asch, Sholem, *The Apostle* (1943); *The Nazarene* (1939).
Deeping, Warwick, *The Cleric's Secret*, The Dial Press, 1944.

Augustine of Hippo (354–430), *Confessions.*
Baxter, Richard, by Frederick J. Powicke (1924).
Beecher, Henry Ward, by Lyman Abbott (1903).
Bunyan, John, by John Brown (1885).
Bushnell, Horace, by Mrs. M. B. Cheney (1903).
Calvin, John, by Williston Walker (1906).
Dale, Robert William, by A. W. W. Dale (1898).
Donne, John, by Izaak Walton (1640).
Drummond, Henry, by George Adam Smith (1898).
Gordon, Charles W. (*Postscript to Adventure: The Autobiography of Ralph Connor* (1938).
Gordon, George A. (*My Education and Religion*) (1925).
Grenfell, Sir Wilfred T. (*A Labrador Doctor*) (1920).
Herbert, George, by Izaak Walton (1670).
Hooker, Richard, by Izaak Walton (1666).

Hughes, Edwin H., Bishop (*I Was Made a Minister*) (1943).
Jowett, John H., by Arthur Porritt (1924).
Kingsley, Charles, by Mrs. Kingsley (1877).
Luther, Martin, by Julius Köstlin (1883).
McCheyne, Robert Murray, by Andrew Bonar.
McLaren, Alexander, by Miss E. T. McLaren (1912).
Moody, Dwight L., by William R. Moody (1930).
Oberlin, Jean F., by Augustus F. Beard (1909).
Rauschenbusch, Walter, by Dores R. Sharpe (1942).
Robertson, Frederick W., by Stopford A. Brooke (2 vols.) (1865).
Robertson, James, by Charles W. Gordon (Ralph Connor) (1908).
Savonarola, by P. Villari (2 vols.) (1887).
Spurgeon, Charles H., by J. C. Carlile (1934).
Truett, George W., by Powhatan W. James (1939).
Watson, John (Ian Maclaren), by Sir William R. Nicoll (1908).
Wesley, John, by Caleb T. Winchester (1922).
Whyte, Alexander, by G. F. Barbour (1923).

Notes

FOREWORD

1. *The Minister: His Life and Work*, p. 194. Abingdon-Cokesbury Press, 1937.
2. *The Minister's Everyday Life*, p. x. Charles Scribner's Sons, 1924.

I

1. *Jesus Christ and the Social Question*, pp. 101, 309. The Macmillian Company, 1900.
2. *Jesus Came Preaching*, p. 115. Charles Scribner's Sons, 1931.
3. *The Servant of the Word*, pp. 92, 124. Charles Scribner's Sons, 1942.
4. Harper & Brothers, 1935.
5. See *The New York Times*, May 18, 1944.
6. *Modern Man in Search of a Soul* (transl.), p. 264. Harcourt, Brace and Company, 1933.
7. See " The Cults: Phenomenon and Challenge," by John E. Kuizenga, in *Theology Today*, April, 1944, pp. 34–46. A brief working bibliography.
8. *How to Be a Pastor*, by Theodore L. Cuyler, p. 20. See also his *Recollections of a Long Life*. Both books published by Baker and Taylor, 1890 and 1902 respectively.

II

1. Pp. 311–314. Abingdon-Cokesbury Press, 1943.
2. See *The Christian Century*, May 10, May 31, 1944, pp. 600, 672.
3. Such work is promoted by *The Council for Clinical Training of Theological Students*, 2 E. 103d Street, New York City. Unfortunately, that organization has enlisted only an occasional seminary student. Expansion will follow World War II.
4. The Macmillan Company, 1936.
5. Willett, Clark & Company, 1939.
6. The Pilgrim Press, 1944.

III

1. *The Poet-Preacher*, p. 27. Methodist Book Concern, 1910.
2. See *The Crisis of Our Age*, by Pitirim A. Sorokin. E. P. Dutton & Co., Inc., 1941.
3. See *The Christ of the American Road*, by E. Stanley Jones. Abingdon-Cokesbury Press, 1944.
4. *Review of Work in 1943*, by Raymond B. Fosdick, President of the Rockefeller Foundation, p. 33. 1944.
5. Charles Scribner's Sons, 1942.
6. The Macmillan Company, 1937; cf. *The Christian Interpretation of Sex*, by Otto A. Piper. Charles Scribner's Sons, 1941.

IV

1. See *George Washington Carver*, by Rackham Holt, p. 105. Doubleday, Doran & Company, Inc., 1943.
2. *Lectures to My Students*, Series II, pp. 164, 165. London, 1877.

V

1. See *Planning a Year's Pulpit Work*, by A. W. Blackwood, Ch. I, " Making the Plan." Abingdon-Cokesbury Press, 1942.
2. *Edwin Arlington Robinson*: A Biography, by Hermann Hagedorn, p. vii. The Macmillan Company, 1938.
3. *Op. cit.*, p. 314.
4. *Talks to Teachers on Psychology*, p. 228. Henry Holt and Company, Inc., 1920.
5. See *Evangelism in the Home Church*, by A. W. Blackwood, Ch. VII, " Special Meetings." Abingdon-Cokesbury Press, 1942.
6. For the other side, read " The Unplanned Life," a sermon by Dean W. L. Sperry, Harvard, in *Rebuilding Our World*, pp. 105–114. Harper & Brothers, 1943.
7. George H. Doran Company, 1908.
8. Jennings and Graham, n.d.
9. Pp. 62–82. Charles Scribner's Sons, 1896.
10. See *The Jesus of History*, by T. R. Glover, pp. 129–133. George H. Doran Company, 1917.
11. *The New Life*, Sermons by Bushnell, pp. 1–15. London, 1892.

12. *The Significance of the Cross,* by F. W. Dillistone, p. 36. The Westminster Press, 1944.

13. *The Poems of Henry van Dyke,* p. 256. Charles Scribner's Sons, 1915.

VII

1. See Gen. 8:22; Isa. 55:10, 11; Matt. 13:1–9, 18–23; Gal. 6:7; *et al.*

2. *Ministerial Ethics and Etiquette,* p. 22. Abingdon-Cokesbury Press, 1928.

IX

1. See *How to Enjoy the Bible,* by Anthony C. Deane. Hodder & Stoughton, Ltd., 1933.

X

1. Third edition, London, 1872, pp. 4, 10, 153, 157, 258, 264.

2. See *Living Under Tension,* pp. 222–232. Harper & Brothers, 1941.

3. *The Table Talk of Martin Luther,* Ch. CCCC, p. 182. Translated and edited by William Hazlitt, London, 1895.

4. *Memoirs of My Life and Thought* (transl.), pp. 59–61. The Macmillan Company, 1925.

XI

1. *How to Deal with Men,* pp. 7–28, *et pass.* London, 1911.

2. See his books: *The Man of God,* Hodder & Stoughton, Ltd., 1935; *The Town Parson,* London, 1919.

3. P. 228. Farrar & Rinehart, Inc., 1943.

4. See I John 2:12–17.

XII

1. This paragraph echoes *An Introduction to Pastoral Theology,* by Henry Balmforth and Others, pp. 164, 165. The Macmillan Company, 1937.

2. For all such matters see *Parish Administration,* by Don F. Fenn. Morehouse-Gorham Company, Inc., 1938.

3. See *The Funeral*, Ch. III, " The Dying Friend," pp. 37–56.
4. *Clerical Errors*, by Louis Tucker, p. 213. Harper & Brothers, 1943.
5. *Old Soldiers Never Die*, by James Ronald, pp. 187, 255, 280. J. B. Lippincott Company, 1942.
6. See *A Manual for Confessors*, by Francis G. Belton (Anglican), pp. 246–249. London, 1931.
7. *Clerical Errors*, p. 178.
8. See the *Memoirs of Thomas Chalmers*, by William Hanna, Vol. I, pp. 305–327. Edinburgh, 1854.

XIII

1. In a statistical bulletin dated April, 1943, the Metropolitan Life Insurance Company reported that the average life of people in the United States had increased almost one third since the beginning of this century.

XIV

1. *Op. cit.*, p. 317.
2. *The Funeral*.
3. By A. V. G. Allen. 3 vols. (also in 2 vols., and in 1 vol.). E. P. Dutton & Company, Inc., 1901.
4. *The Nature and Destiny of Man*. 2 vols. Charles Scribner's Sons, 1941–1943.
5. *The Upper Room*, pp. 92, 93. The Outlook Company, 1903.
6. *Plymouth Pulpit*, First Series, p. 13. J. B. Ford and Company, 1869.

XV

1. *Clerical Errors*, *op. cit.*, pp. 150, 151, 188, 297.
2. See *Planning a Year's Pulpit Work*, pp. 225–231.

XVII

1. Clausen, B. C., *The Technique of a Minister*, p. 22; cf. pp. 15–22. Fleming H. Revell Company, 1925.
2. Smith, Reed, *Learning to Write in College*, p. 5. Little, Brown & Company, 1939.

XVIII

1. *Christian Nurture*, p. 31.
2. The newly revised Methodist *Manual of Worship* is said to include such a set of forms.

XX

1. See *Evangelism in the Home Church.*
2. In his *Yale Lectures on Preaching*, second series (J. B. Ford Company, 1874), he devotes four chapters, 121 pages, to "Revivals."
3. See the *Memoirs and Remains of Robert Murray McCheyne*, by Andrew A. Bonar. Edinburgh, 1892.
4. See *Parish Administration*, by Don F. Fenn. Morehouse-Gorham Company, Inc., 1938.

XXI

1. John 20:24–29, especially v. 28.
2. See *The Gospel for an Age of Doubt*, by Henry van Dyke. The Macmillan Company, 1907.
3. *Henry van Dyke: A Biography*, by Tertius van Dyke, pp. 52, 87. Harper & Brothers, 1935.
4. See *Revivalism in America*, by W. W. Sweet. Charles Scribner's Sons, 1944.
5. *Sermons on Old Testament Characters*, p. 119. Richard R. Smith, 1930.
6. *Pastoral Psychiatry*, Ch. IX. Harper & Brothers, 1938.

XXII

1. *The Minister in the Modern World*, by R. C. Gillie, p. 126. London, 1925.
2. See *The Significance of the Cross*, by F. W. Dillistone, p. 225. The Westminster Press, 1944.
3. See *The Art of Preaching*, p. 14. The Macmillan Company, 1922.
4. See *Method in Soul-Winning*, by Henry C. Mabie, pp. 91, 95. Fleming H. Revell Co., 1906.

5. *Scenes of Clerical Life,* pp. 277, 282, 283, 288, 321, 325. Thomas Y. Crowell Company, n.d.

6. See *The United Church Observer* (Toronto), June 1, 1944, pp. 15, 26.

7. *The Night Is Ending,* by James Roland, p. 383; cf. p. 188. J. B. Lippincott Company, 1944.

8. R. C. Gillie, *op. cit.,* p. 135; cf. II Tim. 3:16, 17.

XXIV

1. P. 90. Whittlesey House, 1942.

2. *Op. cit.,* p. 51.

3. The present writer may seem to be breaking the " rules " by the use of cases. He does not know any other up-to-date method of teaching pastoral theology. He is addressing pastors, not laymen; and he is teaching, not preaching. Even so, he has used discretion in the choice and description of cases.

4. *Op. cit.,* p. 81.

XXV

1. *Charles Kingsley,* by Margaret F. Thorp, pp. 175–181. Princeton University Press, 1943.

2. *The Building of the Church,* pp. 176, 177. The Macmillan Company, 1910.

3. *Op. cit.,* pp. 17, 22, 23, 24–28.

XXVI

1. An Autobiography, pp. 152–161. The Macmillan Company, 1938.

2. *The Philosophy of Loyalty,* by Josiah Royce, p. 16. The Macmillan Company, 1908.

XXVII

1. *Being Made Over* (Sermons), p. 132. Harper & Brothers, 1939.

XXVIII

1. William Hanna, *op. cit.*, I, 305–307.
2. *Ibid.*, I, 472.
3. *The Making of a Minister*, by C. R. Brown, p. 172. The Century Company, 1927.

INDEX

Index of Persons

Administration, Church, Writers on: Beaven, A. W., 53; Cashman, R. W., 130; Clausen, B. C., 138–141, 207; Fenn, Don F., 53, 219; Leach, W. H., 53

Biographies: Drummond, Henry, 231; Gordon, C. W., 231; Gordon, G. A., 231; Keller, Helen, 122; Manning, Cardinal, 134; Mercier, Cardinal, 22; Newman, Cardinal, 231; Partridge, Bellamy, 195; Rauschenbusch, Walter, 232; Robertson, James A., 232; Tucker, Louis, 112, 125; Washington, Booker T., 34

Bishops: Andrewes, Lancelot, 230; Asbury, Francis, 51; Brooks, Phillips (*see* Pastors, U. S. A.); (Finlay, K. G.), 98; Hughes, E. H., 23, 42, 120, 121, 232; (Keeler, S. E.), 37; Quayle, W. A., 28

Counseling, Writers on: Belton, Francis G., 236; Bonnell, J. S., 168; Cameron, W. A., 201; Dexter, E., and R., 193; Dicks, R. L., 20, 115, 119, 201; Dollard, John, 171; Elliott, H. S., and G. L., 171; Gray, A. H., 193, 201; Groves, E. R., 193; Holman, C. T., 171, 184; Jung, C. G., 17, 18; May, Rollo, 201; Peale, N. V., 201; Stolz, K. R., 184; Weatherhead, L. D., 193

Devotional Writers: Andrewes, Lancelot, 230; Augustine of Hippo, 145, 231; Baxter, Richard, 95, 230, 231; Jones, E. S., 119, 234; Speer, R. E., 65, 119; Stewart, George, 76; Suter, J. W., Jr., 76; Taylor, Jeremy, 230

Essayists: Carlyle, Thomas, 41; Royce, Josiah, 211, 238; Ruskin, John, 82

Etiquette, Writers on: Harmon, N. B., Jr., 67; Post, Emily, 62

Evangelists: Asbury, Francis, 51; Moody, D. L., 232; Smith, Gipsy, Sr., 65; Sunday, W. A., 213

Fathers, Church: Ambrose, 230; Augustine, 145, 231; Calvin, John, 141, 202, 231; Chrysostom, 31, 230; Gregory I,

243

230; Luther, Martin, 90, 230, 232; Savonarola, 232; Wesley, John, 202, 232

Missionaries, Abroad: Forsyth, Christina, 134; Grenfell, W. T., 231; Paton, J. G., 145; Schweitzer, Albert, 91; Slessor, Mary, 134

N. T. Characters: Apollos, 209; John, 226; Lydia, 165; Nicodemus, 97; Paul, 26, 33, 80, 101, 117, 154, 163, 209, 230; Peter, 211, 228, 230; Philippian jailer, the, 165; Thomas, 165

Novelists, Abroad: Barrie, J. M., 57, 133, 231; Buchan, John, 133, 216; Carroll, Lewis (Hodgson, C. L.), 151; Crockett, S. R., 231; Cronin, A. J., 95, 231; Deeping, Warwick, 231; Doyle, A. C., 216; Eliot, George (Marian Evans), 25, 168, 179, 196, 231; Goldsmith, Oliver, 230; Hughes, Thomas, 133; Hugo, Victor, 95, 231; Macdonald, George, 231; Oliphant, Mrs. Margaret, 231; Roland, James, 181; Trollope, Anthony, 95, 231; Walpole, Hugh, 231; Ward, Mrs. Humphry, 231

Novelists, U. S. A.: Asch, Sholem, 231; Deland, Mrs. Margaret, 231; Douglas, L. C., 9, 194, 231; Glasgow, Ellen, 68; Gordon, C. W., 231; King, Basil, 231; Lewis, Sinclair, 231; Skinner, C. O., 133; Stowe, H. B., 231

O. T. Characters: David, 78; Elijah, 164; Job, 170; Nehemiah, 204

Pastoral Work, Writers on: Adams, Hampton, 70; Bader, Mrs. J. M. (ed.), 60; Balmforth, Henry, 235; Brown, C. R., 40, 215, 221; Cabot and Dicks, 103, 133, 136; Calkins, Raymond, 20, 24, 86, 101; Cunningham, William, 27; Erdman, C. R., 40; Gillie, R. C., 176; Gladden, Washington, 40; Green, Peter, 83, 94, 205, 206; Hewitt, A. W., 24, 60; Jefferson, C. E., 205, 224, 229; Johnson, Mrs. A. F., 60; Leavell, R. Q., 161; McAfee, C. B., 33; Palmer, A. W., 33; Pleune, Peter, 70; Sherrill, L. J., 93; Trumbull, C. G., 161; Underhill, Francis (ed.), 33

Pastors, Abroad: Andrews, C. F., 177; Chalmers, Thomas, 95, 114, 220, 223, 231; Dale, R. W., 208, 231; Farrar, F. W.,

Index of Subjects

Index of Cases

Dr. Paul Rees – "Movies and the Conscientious Christian"
Rice – "Whats wrong with the Movies"
Wimberly
Dan Gilbert

Henry Forthmen "our Movie Made Children
(psychologist's standpoint)
  not ethical or moral.
     hinders sleep
     Lowers Ideals –
     Exhaults sin."

Objections → profit
1. Motive – profit
2. People who act
3. Places they are shown
4. contrast
        Educational films
            and
     Commercial   "

122 – on death + eternal life
            Hope + love